This book contains original stories by Kelsey Guetschow and Christoph Trappe, dba Trappe Digital LLC. Copies are available on Amazon in paperback and for Kindle. You also may order signed or group orders by contacting us here: AuthenticStorytelling.net/contact-us.

To request permission to republish parts of our stories, please contact us here: AuthenticStorytelling.net/contact-us.

Contents

About the Authors 7

Introduction 9

Getting Started 11

    Yes, it's always about us 11

    Customer experience: the battleground 14

    Online/offline scheduling integration can work 19

    It got personal: when a 'patient experience' became my experience 21

    Customer feedback can be easy: So why do we make it so hard? 25

    Selling versus collaborating: it can be the same 28

    ROI crazy talk: How is this 'being nice' thing helping the bottom line? 30

    The words we choose matter 32

    Compassion goes a long way 33

How to Know You Are Customer-Centric 36

    Experience recall: Do your customers remember? . 36

Making decisions based on personal likes is not customer-centric..39

How can somebody who knows everything be customer-centric?...40

What's with all the paperwork? 42

Optimize your content for relevance........................43

Refocusing on Why We Do What We Do 46

Shifting a leadership focus to service 46

It's the little things that make (or break) the customer experience 50

Decisions should benefit the end user 53

Some companies delight customers..........................55

Context and perspective: just another tumor, cancer, gunshot wound … 61

Know your purpose..68

Be transparent with your customers........................71

People Need to Be Customer-Centric 75

Being nice...75

Digital strategists can be customer advocates 78

Leadership focus: Help customers convert more, work less, and enjoy the experience 83

Making things easy should be easy 90

Barriers to Being Customer-Centric 91

The pressure of perfection in social media 91

When creating a lovely customer experience leaves a bigger impact on you 97

Some audiences need different things 103

Scripts can hurt customer service 105

Inconveniences are unavoidable: How you respond matters 108

Apply empathy: It benefits your business and your customer 111

Automation and Technology: Customer-Centric or Not? 115

Automation isn't always good 115

Your automation is working when customers don't notice 117

A dictated medical note transformed how I view doctor-patient communication 122

Personalization by geography doesn't always work well.. 128

Mass communication: customer-centric or not? ... 130

How disruptive 132

Testing can help us be customer-centric 133

How A/B testing might go away 135

Testing: good for business, better for the customer
.... 138

How many emails is too many? 142

How to Prove Success 146

Measuring the wrong thing 146

Measure what matters, not everything you can 150

Interact with your organization like you are a customer 152

Payoff for Doing It Well 157

Long-term payoff 157

Unexpected benefits of great customer experience 158

Getting reviews 162

Even more online communication issues 169

Measuring success 171

Creating customer advocates 173

Conclusion 176

About the Authors

Kelsey Guetschow (The Thoughtful Strategist)

Kelsey blogs at TheThoughtfulStrategist.com. When not blogging, she travels coast to coast sharing poignant digital strategy, healthcare business tactics, and perspectives on women in business and technology. Her distinctive background as a service-academy graduate, Air Force hospital administrator, and war veteran uniquely influences her perspective on business – and makes for some colorful stories. This is Kelsey's first book.

Book her to speak: guetschowk@gmail.com

Connect with Kelsey:

- Twitter: @kguetschow
- Web: TheThoughtfulStrategist.com
- Email: guetschowk@gmail.com

Christoph Trappe (The Authentic Storyteller)

This is Christoph Trappe's second book and part two in his authentic storytelling content marketing book series. *Get Real: Sharing Authentic Stories for Long-term Success* published in late 2015. His third book on the emerging role of content marketing journalists is in the planning stages.

Christoph blogs at AuthenticStorytelling.net and frequently flies around the globe to share message of authenticity, being real, and being helpful.

Book him to speak: ctrappe@christophtrappe.com.

Connect with Christoph:

- Twitter: @ctrappe
- Web: AuthenticStorytelling.net
- Email: ctrappe@christophtrappe.com

Introduction

Two marketers walk into a restaurant on a date. They instantly convert each other.

It's all about the conversion. How can we get you, our customer, to do what we want you to do? Mostly, we want you to give us your money.

- Click here to buy something.
- Sign up for our newsletter here. By the way, I need your home address and phone number to send you an email. In actuality, I just want that information so I can send you more marketing things to convince you to spend money more quickly. Please continue buying and tell your friends to buy. Oh, and the emails won't stop.
- I know you want this product, so let me charge you an arm and a leg. There's a convenience charge and another for the processing and handling. Does the up-charging thing ever stop?

Marketing tactics can get out of hand, as you may imagine. Don't get us wrong. We're all for making money, but as Tim O'Reilly, Founder and CEO of O'Reilly Media, has said, "Money is like gasoline during a road trip. You don't want to run out of gas on your trip, but you aren't doing a tour of gas stations."

Really, our road trip is about the experience. So are our lives. Everything we do, create, or sell comes back to: how do we add to our experiences and those of others?

That's why we're writing this book focused on how organizations can be more customer-centric, why you need to, how to know if you are, and how to measure your success at creating experiences that foster long-term, loyal, and satisfied customers.

As co-authors, we bring vastly different backgrounds and perspectives to these chapters. Kelsey, a former military officer works with hospitals around the United States on large-scale, technical website projects, approaches customer experience primarily through the digital landscape and shares universal lessons through the lens of healthcare. She includes personal stories and insights from wartime, hospitals, and customer digital experiences.

Christoph brings his storytelling angle to the discussion from years in journalism and marketing. He understands the power of the authentic story and shares how companies must leverage their personal connections to customers to refine their experiences.

Let's get started.

Getting Started

Yes, it's always about us
By Christoph

One of the reasons it's so hard to be customer- or user-centric is that most of the time the customer or user isn't us.

And it's always about us. We know us. We see life from our own perspective. That sounds selfish – because it kind of is. But that's life.

Even people who claim it's not about them get something out of doing something for others.

It's OK, and we can accept it. No need to argue over who is more and who is less selfish. We know ourselves the best because we are around ourselves the most – like all the time. Ha.

This is important to remember, though, for those of us who work with customers and build digital experiences for users. For the most part, we are not typical customers or users ourselves.

It's hard to remember that. But when we keep in mind that it's about the customer and why it's good to make the experience about them, we can succeed.

In customer service, for example, the better we serve the customer, the better it will be for us. Happy customers are likely to give us more money, referrals, etc.

Downtown Tire in Cedar Rapids, Iowa, comes to mind as an example. They always find time to help when my car has issues. Always. Once I had a car problem at 4:45, and they squeezed me in before closing time – which is at 5:30. It's a big differentiator from the shops that require you to book days out.

Not being selfish is good for Downtown Tire as I, and many others, keep going back and freely and happily recommend them. They don't even ask us to refer friends, but people do it because Downtown Tire is awesome with customer service and car repairs.

Designing digital experiences is similar. There are still way too many websites that try to make visitors do things that are only good for the website's owner:

- Look at the flashing ad.
- Did you see it?
- CLICK IT!
- Answer these questions for the privilege to read our below-average content.
- Here's a popup. I know you just got here, but do these things for me now.

The problem with annoying techniques is that they work just enough for organizations to continue using them. Again, it's about me – the organization – and not the customer. People don't recommend crappy website experiences to their friends. But they might share a great new scheduling tool or a new shopping site.

Let's be selfish for our customers and end users first, and it'll end up being good for them and us. But it's a balance. Let's not get crazy and say, "The customer is always right, even when he's not." Blah blah blah. Sounds wrong to me.

Nobody is always right, and being customer-centric is not about agreeing with everything a customer claims to be fact.

Being customer-centric is about providing the best customer experience at every moment – even when it's not a completely positive one, and even when we have to disagree with a customer. Examples include when something simply can't be done, something will cost more, or a timeline was set too tightly to be met.

The key is to provide a top-notch experience to the customer, to make them feel valued and understood, and have them walk away with a great feeling, even when things didn't turn out perfectly.

I've had negative experiences before with organizations, but the way they handled them still made me feel good. It's about listening and responding, and sometimes making it up through something free.

When customers walk away and share stories of experiences they felt were worth passing on, that's a sign that the organization is customer-centric.

When customers feel like we value their time and see that we do our best to help them with their specific problem, that's customer-centric.

When we are customer-centric, our positive authentic stories will be shared far and wide by customers. But keep in mind that when we aren't customer-centric our stories will be shared as well – except they won't be glowing endorsements.

Customer experience: the battleground
By Kelsey

"Customer experience is the next competitive battleground. It's where business is going to be won or lost." – Tom Knighton, author of *Managing the Customer Experience.*

The small things make all the difference, and creating a lovely customer experience can leave a lasting impact on you. You can make these impacts with a customer in person – when you have the opportunity to interact with them. This layer of customer experience is critical to creating long-term relationships.

In today's digital age, the first touchpoint of a customer experience is rarely in person. It is usually through the web or an app. Excluding some retail and restaurants, almost all businesses' first touchpoints for customer experience are online. Welcome to the digital age! Well, a digital age that, in truth, has been here for quite some time...

When talking to organizations, I often use the adage, "Google is your new front door." In some cases, it has even replaced a call center, a traditional first touchpoint for many organizations.

How do you find a doctor today? Google it. How do you learn more about treating a [fill in disease here]? Google it. What does it mean when you have a [fill in symptom here]? Google it.

So, since most patients likely start their healthcare journey with Google, MD, your website needs to:

1) Be found in search engines to meet those customers' needs, and,

2) Be easy to use once that patient is trying to take the "next step."

Now, No. 1 can be met through search engine optimization of the website – a more technical approach. But we also need to make the digital experience easy for your customers to take the next step. Please don't make your customers work to give you their business.

Customer interaction with a health system should be fluid, hassle-free, straightforward, and welcoming, *especially* online.

Organizational politics bog down progress within many industries, especially healthcare. You have marketing, physician groups, nurse managers, IT, administrators, and more, all battling over whose priorities should take precedence in internal processes, in social media, and on a website. No wonder healthcare is an industry accused of being a "slow adapter" into anything related to digital.

Luckily, digital has an advantage – it is closely tied to data. I love data. It (almost) takes the politics out of conversations. As digital agency owner Andy Crestodina has said: You can't bring opinions to a data fight. Instead, find out what works, what doesn't, and adjust your approach to maximize your organizational impact and market momentum.

For example, consider lengthy online contact forms. When a user sees one, they're likely to think, "Wow, that's a long form," and leave the website.

More and more healthcare organizations are establishing online appointment engagement opportunities. Most organizations are still asking users to "submit a form and we'll call you back." Frequently used as conversion points for marketing campaigns, forms are used throughout a website – customers can submit a form and receive a call back with an appointment scheduled for a requested date and time of day. Or, through growing adaptation of electronic medical records, people schedule their own appointments online in real time.

A general web usability rule is that shorter forms, which make for an easier customer experience, get filled out more. If you break down barriers in the way of a customer accomplishing a task, they're more likely to make that conversion. Unnecessary fields in forms often are those barriers.

When working with clients to simplify the customer experience, I often hear responses like, "No, the call center has to have all that information to call the patient back." From working as a hospital administrator, I understand this is the case in some instances. However, one of my roles during that time was managing a call center, and I also know it's rarely a true requirement.

When your organization struggles to justify a customer experience improvement, use data to help bolster your change management initiative.

Here's an example of a simple form test: cut the number of fields required for submission for form version A by *two fields* (a tiny change!) and funnel half of the traffic to view the new form. I used this approach, watched for two weeks as thousands of users moved throughout the site, and reported back the results of the simple test.

As expected, the drop off rate, which is defined by how many people started at least one field of the form and exited without completing it, stayed exactly the same.

However, the completion rate (how many people came to the page and completed the form) rose by 4 percent. This is a small number – but remember, we made a really small change. Regardless, 4 percent more patient leads can mean millions in revenue over the course of a year.

Cutting the length of one by 50 percent the drop-off rate decreased by 2 percent, but the completion rate increased by 10 percent!

In the end, using data to work with internal teams to optimize the customer experience contributed to more leads. Win, win.

The patient experience is what matters, in person and online. Making small changes to usher patients into your health system creates a much nicer patient experience. In the end, it also helps them easily convert into a customer – and I have yet to hear a business complain about having too many customers.

Customers expect full integration across all channels. I expect to be able to reach companies through online means – whether through social media, their websites, or traditional email. I expect organizations to pay attention when I reach out to them. Thank you if your organization pays attention on all channels. If yours doesn't, it's time to start.

Online/offline scheduling integration can work
By Christoph

Jumping off of Kelsey's comments about connecting with patients online …

Being available and transparent about when experts are available is a sign of good customer service, which naturally leads to a positive patient experience. The same principles apply to both.

Here's an example. I was stopping by a store on a Saturday afternoon to get new glasses. I've gone to the same eye doctor for a number of years and had no plans to switch. But I took my prescription to my local Target store to get new glasses – mostly because they were convenient on a Saturday afternoon. I wanted to go then, and they were open.

I also went because my wife had scheduled an eye appointment at that same store earlier in the day. She'd texted that they were having a 25 percent off sale. That helped, too, in making my decision. When I arrived at the store, I saw a sign with the schedule of openings. Though I still had to go online to schedule an appointment, it was great to see what times were available. Plus, the sign at the store for all to see was a great advertising tool.

I thought it was a fantastic way to integrate the different channels by alerting passersby:

- That the store offers eye exams
- When there were openings
- That online scheduling was available

I mentioned the sign to my wife and shared some of these points with her, which prompted her to say, "Oh yeah, of course I scheduled my appointment online."

There are still plenty of organizations across many industries that are not fully integrated across all channels customers use online and offline. And sometimes the channels change. One gets added and one gets subtracted. The relevant masses decide what channels should be important.

Often, the reason I hear that full-channel integration is not there yet is because the current setup is working. And that might be true – it is working just well enough. We're making enough money, we have enough customers, and the business is going well. But it could be going even better when we fully integrate channels.

Integration across all channels shows a customer-centric approach. Organizations that respond on Twitter, that let me book or schedule online, and that respond to my phone calls show what true customer service is about. Thank you to all who are doing this for your customers and making our lives easier.

It got personal: when a 'patient experience' became my experience
By Kelsey

When I was first brainstorming a name for my blog, many of the ideas revolved around the idea of "experience." The Thoughtful Strategist blog remains focused on experience – authentic experience, to be precise. Experience is a lens through which I constantly evaluate the effectiveness and success of any interaction between a patient and a health system. Does it create the experience intended for the patient? Experience transcends healthcare; it applies to all industries. Organizations use billions of marketing dollars to align their brand, product, service, etc., to the customer experience.

In healthcare, customer experience is a patient experience. For a pediatric patient, that experience extends to the engagement with the child and their family members. Creating that multidimensional experience is a much more complex process in clinical and inpatient environments. In 2016, I had the opportunity to see how it can be done extremely well.

Unfortunately, my 10-month-old son came down with a bad bug. He couldn't keep food down all weekend, and severe dehydration landed us in the ER on a Monday morning. After some anti-nausea medication and more fluids, we were discharged. But by that evening, my son was laboring to breathe. On Tuesday afternoon, we were back in the doctor's office and immediately admitted to the University of Iowa Children's Hospital. Over the next four days he got worse. Every day was a new tube, a higher level of respiratory support, and additional measures of care with no improvement. On day four, he spiked a high fever. As we were preparing for a move to the pediatric intensive care unit, he took a turn for the better within an hour. Finally! It was another long few days, but not as scary as the first part of our visit.

What an experience for my son, my husband, me. The hospital had a number of customers to serve during our time in the hospital, and the team did it very well, focusing on the little things that made a big difference during a challenging time. The providers, nurses, medical assistants, and housekeeping personnel were helpful, considerate, thorough, and supportive.

For example, when we were waiting to be transferred from the outpatient office to the inpatient unit, instead of sending us to the ER to wait for a bed to be ready, they had us stay in the comfortable exam room and frequently checked on us during our hour wait. The residents brought us water and snacks and gave my son a book to help keep him occupied. Before they sent us to the inpatient floor, they provided us a "fast-track" sheet to expedite our admission to the inpatient floor.

When we arrived, we were immediately ushered into a clean, private room and walked through what would happen next. Throughout our stay, the medical and administrative team did an excellent job performing their job through the lens of serving their customers in room 2JCP44 – all three of us.

In-person experience is the core of customer service and the focus of clinical management. But what about the rest of the touchpoints a customer interacts with when they communicate with your organization? Are they as personal? As refined and welcoming? In the world of web and digital, the same customer experience rules apply.

When a customer submits a contact form on your website, do they get a thank you message for submitting their form? Or is there a nicer, personal message that explains when they should be hearing back from a representative who is looking forward to helping them? And do you offer another touchpoint, such as an invitation to read your blog, review your services, or call you for assistance?

In general, organizations struggle to create the same personal experiences in a digital environment. But that space is exactly where they make the biggest difference, setting you apart and creating a customer relationship from your very first engagement.

Customer feedback can be easy: So why do we make it so hard?

By Kelsey

Asking customers what they think is easy – in theory. How many times do you get a receipt from a clothing or retail store and the bottom half of the receipt says something like, "We care what you think. Fill out our survey for a chance to win $500"? Or, you're on hold and get the prompt to "press one" to take a quick survey at the end of the call?

Businesses inundate customers with the opportunity to provide feedback on their experience. The market for customer feedback is saturated to the point of ineffectiveness. We have to approach collecting customer feedback differently if we really want to know how we can improve.

In one of my experiences, providing customer feedback wasn't worth a chicken sandwich promised on the receipt. I took one of those surveys a few months ago for the first time ever. Well, let me rephrase, I started to take one of those surveys.

My husband and I were on a brief, irregular, hour-long "date." It was unglamorous – we had headed to the mall to get some errands done at Target and eat at

Chick-fil-A. Nevertheless, any hour away on our own classified as a fabulous date, considering we had a colicky infant at home. We finished our meal, and the receipt included a link to take a survey, promising a free chicken sandwich if we told them about our experience. Since my husband was driving home, I pulled up the survey on my phone. This would be an easy $3 saved on our next trip to the mall, right? Wrong.

The first page of the survey was about 10 questions long. Three pages later and only 18 percent complete, I gave up. If they really cared about my experience, why were they making it so hard to collect the feedback? Disclosure: I do like Chick-fil-A as an organization. I especially appreciate initiatives like their 2016 family challenge where they provide a box to stash your cell phones, creating an electronics-free family mealtime. However, as much as I appreciate some of their initiatives, I still won't be taking their incredibly long survey to let them know.

If businesses need to know how happy they're making their customers and identify areas for continual improvement, it's critical for long-term success to collect the data to inform those adjustments. Performing these assessments also has to be done with customer-centric methods.

In 2016, I was flying back from a conference in Orlando. There was a kiosk outside of the tram station at the airport. It was a simple stand with a sign that said, "Please rate your checkpoint wait time." It had four colored buttons: green, yellow, orange, and red. The buttons had transitioning happy faces on them, starting with a smiling green button and ending with a sad red button. It was cute and catchy. The concept was simple.

As the tram pulled up, I pressed a button and provided my feedback on the experience. I liked the idea and appreciated how they were making it fun.

As a marketer and thought leader who focuses on customer experience and discovering ways to improve business touch points, I loved how data was collected quickly and could be compared to time of day, tram schedules, flight schedules, and so on. Lastly, and most importantly, it was easy for the customer. This fun interaction removed barriers to customer engagement.

If we really want to know what our customers think so we can better serve them (and increase ROI), we have to make it easy for them to tell us.

Selling versus collaborating: it can be the same
By Kelsey

I had a conversation in May 2016 that, at its core, revolved around communicating value of a product a customer had purchased already. One of the participants said, "I'm not sales-y, so I can't talk about it [a digital product] like that." I was surprised by this description of the organization/customer conversation.

I don't consider traditional "sales" to be one of my strengths. I'm not a schmoozer, and in fact, I still consider negotiations a personal weakness of sorts. However, I never thought of these customer conversations as "sales-y." Why? I wasn't trying to sell the customer anything that 1) they didn't already purchase (the meeting was a demo to share the value of what they bought) or 2) wouldn't benefit them by making their customer experience better.

In essence, the products I shared were helpful. They could be a valuable addition to increase efficiency, solve a problem, or increase ROI.

When I think of stereotypical sales people, I think of a trickster – someone trying to get me to buy something that I don't need, doesn't work as advertised, and is significantly overpriced. I picture the stereotypical used car salesman trying to sell off a lemon to an unwitting customer.

The experience of being that employee, trying to sell something that is not valuable to a customer, is uncomfortable. It feels icky, for lack of a more sophisticated term. But it shouldn't. If you establish mutual trust and always operate in the best interest of the customer, it's a good experience for you both.

My approach to any customer conversation has always been to learn what they need so I can make a recommendation to make their experience, and their business, better. We all should be having these types of interactions with customers: talking through what problems we can help solve, what is working well, and how we can help support their goals by solving those problems and bolstering their strengths.

Equally as important is being able to tell a customer a product won't support their needs or to recommend they go in a different direction. Be transparent. It builds trust, advocacy, and long-term loyalty. And an added bonus: You maintain integrity throughout the engagement (and there is nothing icky about that!).

When you genuinely care about bettering your customers' lives, it changes engagements from tepid skepticism to mutual collaboration. Selling and collaborating happen in the same conversation when you approach the customer with the intent to better their business.

Focusing on the value you create for your customers transforms those relationships. In the end, focusing on value makes it stickier and, more often than not, builds the foundation for a long-term partnership.

ROI crazy talk: How is this 'being nice' thing helping the bottom line?
By Christoph

The impact of "being nice" can be hard to measure, yet I can assure you that people stop spending money with businesses that aren't nice:

- When you are greeted by a guy behind the counter who is cranky because you got there at 8:59 and they open at 9:00.
- When the customer service rep you were on hold with doesn't call back when the phone call was dropped by mistake.
- When it appears that you – the customer – are an inconvenience. Sorry for stopping by. Yikes.

The other day, I dropped my car off at an auto shop I don't normally use to get a remote starter installed. Hey, I live in Iowa and it gets -30 degrees or so in the winter here! I was trying to work nearby, but the closest gas station unfortunately had no tables or chairs.

I instead decided to go to a nearby McDonald's to work, even though I really didn't want to do that. Though you can drive through to get your food, I even try to avoid doing that.

Anyway, I did get a coffee and a snack, and the person behind the counter said, "Go ahead, have a seat, and get situated. I'll bring this out when it's ready."

Wait, they do that at McDonald's? She brought it out with a smile. Then when I was finished and working with laptop in front of me, she stopped by again and said, "All done? Let me take that out of your way."

What's the ROI of her being so nice? Anyone got the formula? I even left a positive review for that particular McDonald's on Facebook. I was pleasantly surprised by the service and the positive attitude was awesome. Turns out others at that McDonald's were similarly nice, and not just to me. They smiled, even when they were mopping the floor.

I'm a big fan of measuring things and seeing progress. Don't get me wrong. Heck, I measure my daily steps, sleep, and calories burned.

But sometimes we overthink things. What's the ROI of being nice? I would like to rephrase that: What's the negative impact of not being nice?

The words we choose matter
By Christoph

Customer service comes from the inside and from the top down. If it's not a business priority from the leadership team, it won't be for the frontline team.

The words we choose show if we are customer- and user-centric. Here's an example.

For some time, I've been a member of an organization I like very much and use extensively. When the time came for us to switch membership levels, we met with one of their staff members. The employee walked us through the changes, fees, and everything, and said, "We don't get to charge you this enrollment fee because you are already a member."

I wondered, is it all about getting to charge me more? It was a good reminder that the words we choose signal what we are really about.

I wouldn't be surprised if behind-the-scenes discussions focus more on how much to charge people and when as opposed to what the best plans are for people. I certainly could be wrong, but that's the perception his statements gave me. We will make you give us your money for being a member. We get to.

Now in this case, it didn't make any difference to our relationship as we still renewed. But long term, it can. We might switch when we run across a similar organization that has a more customer-centric mission that is displayed through words and actions.

This concept certainly applies to digital strategy. Are we focused on being truly helpful or just constantly selling? The words we use behind the scenes to discuss client relations and strategy impact how we interact with clients directly.

It also applies when it comes to creating products like websites that are going to be used by consumers. Are we really keeping the users' needs in mind, or are we being organization-centric? It's easy to focus on our needs since we know them. But focusing on the end user actually will help us be more successful. It can be a long-term differentiator.

Compassion goes a long way
By Kelsey

A few weeks ago, my husband came home from working an Emergency Room (ER) shift. We started talking about the culture within the ER. Traditionally, there are long wait times for patients, minimal amenities, and people aren't there because they feel great and can't wait to take on the day. It's usually concerning life, limb, eyesight, or in my case, a pair of first-time parents with a 10-month-old whose fever and food won't stay down. It's also often in the middle of the night – our last visit was around 3:30 a.m. Not a great recipe for a wonderful patient experience in any healthcare setting.

As we ate dinner together, he told me that there was a young parent who had been in the ER with her sick baby since 1 a.m. He saw her around 10 a.m. to see if the consulting sub-service had seen her yet. She couldn't order food (since she wasn't the patient), but he had worked with the nurses to get her a food voucher and pick up a meal (since she couldn't leave her infant in the room or take the baby with her).

Before I go on, please note: I don't share this to tout what a lovely, thoughtful man I ingeniously married years ago. Or to pretend we have deep, intellectual conversations all of the time (within 5 minutes we were discussing our son's stool consistency to determine if he would get banana for dessert).

What struck me was his observation about the shift in his own mindset as a healthcare provider for his patients. He said, "When you approach your patients as people and find ways to show compassion, it changes the interaction. I like finding ways to make their stay a little bit better. Whether it was getting that parent food, holding a patient's hand and talking to her about her children while she's having her broken leg evaluated, or bringing in some water, it all goes a long way."

Healthcare is the ultimate service industry – the stakes are higher than in any other. You impact health, wellness, lives, longevity, or death by the kind of service you provide. Human beings can be at their worst when they are vulnerable. And when are you more vulnerable than when you can't control your own life? When you're completely reliant on others to take care of you, make you better, and bring you back to health?

During these times of vulnerability, compassion matters more than ever. Taking a few extra minutes to identify how you can positively affect a patient's experience makes all the difference. Shift your mindset to see patients or customers as individuals with stories and fears or challenges that you can help alleviate during each interaction. This makes it easier to show compassion – and compassion goes a long way.

How to Know You Are Customer-Centric

Experience recall: Do your customers remember?

By Kelsey

Being customer-centric is a business philosophy that can permeate attitudes around how you approach your customers and employees. Do your customers remember you? And if so, do they remember you for the right reasons?

I was at lunch with colleagues in February 2016, and we were discussing a bonus buget – essentially extra budget a company can reserve to do the things to make a client's experience nicer and complete. In some cases, it goes to fix something without cost to the client, but it is intended to be used to deliver "delighters" – the additional touches that polish the experience.

As we moved on to another topic, the server brought dessert. She passed around everyone's individual orders and then brought an additional portion of chocolate bread pudding. When she delivered it, she said, "This is the dessert we are really known for, and I wanted to be sure you all could try it today. I hope you enjoy it." We dug in – it was lovely! The server used her bonus budget to delight our table. In turn, she created a memorable experience. The next time I return to that restaurant, I will be ordering the chocolate bread pudding and I remember that free dessert whenever I think of that restaurant.

The same kind of associative recall applies to digital experiences. Is your website hard to use or easy to navigate? Users will remember the experience of struggling to find the right phone number to call – next time, they may call your competitor or rely on web search results in lieu of using your site. That's not the kind of recall you want to impress upon your customers.

I flew with Delta a few times last year. In one instance, we were slightly delayed due to weather. Other than that, it was travel as normal. I did not think twice about the delay because it was due to a snowstorm and all of the outbound flights were delayed one to three hours. Our flight crew was hustling to get us off the ground as soon as possible, and I appreciated the sense of urgency after a long day of meetings.

However, a day after I returned, I received an email from Delta with a quick rating request about their service during the delay. Here is a snippet from the email:

"Dear Kelsey,

We noticed that you experienced a delay on March 01, 2016. We are very sorry for the delay. As a valued SkyMiles member, your feedback is important to us and will help us continue to improve. We ask that you please provide feedback on your experience by answering the questions below."

An airline asking for my feedback? Especially around a delay that was unavoidable for all airlines at that airport? I was surprised. The experience left an impact – Delta cares about my experience, and they value their customers' feedback. It was an impressive touch.

Both the email and the free dessert were memorable experiences. They were sticky.

The impact of an experience aids in a customer's "experience recall." This is the emotional impression on your customer and often the first thing they go to when recalling their interaction with your company. Yes, they may remember the things that did not go well, but when the balance of the experience is skewed to the positive, often it's the unexpected delighters that have the potential to leave the longest-lasting impression. In those cases, your customers will have a more positive experience recall to share with others.

Making decisions based on personal likes is not customer-centric
By Christoph

You may have heard this before: We have to change a graphic/website/whatever because the boss doesn't like it.

And why doesn't the boss like it? Who knows. He didn't tell us. He doesn't have to. He's the boss. What year is this? Ha.

Personal preference is an unacceptable reason to withhold something from a specific audience. Our preference might not be the same as our audience's preference.

Personal preferences aren't going away because, well, they're our opinions. But we should remember that personal likes or dislikes might not reflect what will work best for a specific audience.

Certainly, some audience-centric decisions are educated guesses, even when we have data. But at the very least, when we put the audience first and verbally discuss what might be best for them, we are trying to be audience-centric versus organization-centric.

So, what can you do when somebody says an item needs to change because they don't like it? Gently ask,

"Can you tell me more?" Do your part to work with your team to ensure a positive experience for your customers.

How can somebody who knows everything be customer-centric?
By Christoph

Some people claim they know everything. And they believe it! I don't think that people who believe they know everything can be truly customer-centric. Let me give you an example.

Once I was part of a conversation with three other guys. One worked for some mechanical-type company and the second guy had hired him to install something at his home. The customer told the mechanical worker that whatever was installed wasn't working, and he needed his help.

The mechanical worker (the apparent expert) got into this big monologue over how the problem couldn't have been caused by the installation, and they'd have to do something completely different because there was just no way that he'd done something wrong.

Of course, the customer looked like he was just put in his place. "Ummm, OK." He knew for sure that he didn't know what was wrong, and he also knew that whatever the mechanical worker did wasn't working.

The third guy chimed in, directing his comment at the mechanical worker, "This is the 21st century, you know. There likely are options."

But the mechanical worker couldn't be convinced. He just knew he was right without even looking at what was going on.

Now, he might have been right. I don't know. See? I don't know everything either. At the very least, it was not a good customer experience.

The customer-centric way to handle a situation like this is to:

- Acknowledge the customer's frustration and problem.
- Ask some clarifying questions.
- Offer some expert opinion, such as, "In the past, here's what has happened." But don't present it so strongly that it shuts the door for further discussion, which doesn't feel good to the customer.
- Explain all the options and associated costs.
- Extend an offer to fix whatever is wrong, which in this case likely would include visiting the customer's home again.

Customer-centric doesn't mean that we can't have opinions or aren't the experts in our specialized areas. We can and should be – people hire other people for their expertise. But we do have to make it feel good and be a positive experience for customers, even when negative reasons prompt the situation.

What's with all the paperwork?
By Christoph

When I interview with potential partners or shop around for new services, sometimes I get this response: Let me email you more information.

And then they do. And it's like 20 pages. Single spacing. Size 10 font. OK, now I'm just being overly dramatic. But seriously, if you can't explain it to me in a sentence or two, how can you expect me to understand the important basics to start a new partnership or buy anything?

People probably skim the information anyway. Who has time to read all that stuff? Besides, it's not very customer-friendly. If you can't explain it to me, how will I be able to explain it to my wife or business partners? Even if I have the final say, I still like to bounce ideas off trusted people.

Customer-centric organizations and marketers don't make customers think. They also don't exploit them with unnecessary paperwork or terms of service that cover everything down to how my dog can use a new app on my phone. Seriously!

They may ask questions to get more information about what problems customers are trying to solve or what their goals are. Then customer-centric people will present a simple answer and, if there are options, they might present up to three. Yes, I know, most likely will pick the middle option, but it's simple at least.

In our attention-starved days, who has time to dig deep into research at the early stages? I know I don't. Explain the basics and be helpful. Explaining things simply can set you apart.

Optimize your content for relevance
By Christoph

We won't be talking about black hat tips or strategies that annoy consumers here. We want to be found through authentic storytelling and relevant content marketing by people who want to engage with and buy from us.

Even if we are "just" blogging and have no actual product to ship out, we still are selling an experience. People pay by consuming and sharing our content and talking positively about us.

In the content marketing (authentic storytelling) world, we should focus on optimizing our content. Yes. I mean it. But we should optimize it to be more relevant. How do we make the content as clear as it can be, use the words our audience uses, and actually help them solve their problems?

And we should avoid making people jump through hoops. For example, we shouldn't make visitors who use smart phones fill out forms that are not optimized for mobile. And we shouldn't make them download forms as non-optimized PDFs. That's a hoop, and one that doesn't even work on mobile.

Here's my list of the best ways to optimize your content for maximum impact:

1. Make a list of topics that you actually have something to say about, and bonus if you're passionate about them.
2. Research what people are Googling in relation to your topics. Nope, you are not going to use this data to keyword stuff articles. You can use it to find out what questions people are seeking

    answers to on the web and write articles to provide those answers.
3. Be honest, human, truthful, responsive, and authentic. Share personal stories that offer value to the people you're trying to reach.
4. Share blog posts on a schedule. Maybe start with once or twice a week.
5. Promote your content. Print business cards for your blog and hand them out at events – anywhere it's relevant offline! Allow people to get posts by email. Share your posts on social media, but don't post just links. Offer relevant tidbits without links, too, to showcase your expertise and thought leadership. Make sure your site has share buttons on every post so others can share your content and help it spread.
6. Look at your metrics and see what's working. But don't check them every two minutes. Content strategies almost always require several months to take off.

Optimizing content is important. Doing it right helps people find it. Get there by sharing authentic stories that can help, inform, and educate. And, of course, share your stories in a constant, consistent, and relevant way.

Refocusing on Why We Do What We Do

Shifting a leadership focus to service
By Kelsey

When you approach your work through the lens of how to best serve your customers, so much falls into place.

Ancient philosophers such as Lao-Tzu described servant leadership, and Robert K. Greenleaf coined the modern phrase in "The Servant as Leader," an essay he first published in 1970. The term is used throughout industry and leadership disciplines. All organizations within service industries focus on "service," and in healthcare, the kind of service a patient receives usually carries more weight than their experience within a retail store, for example.

The healthcare experience is serious. I would argue that it's more important than the experience of a vacation or restaurant. The service a doctor, nurse, technician, or administrator provides in the healthcare setting can be the difference between life or death, long-term discomfort or a quick recovery, peace of mind or added stress, and ease of access or a lengthy wait.

So, yes, service is important. The quality, timeliness, and technology of service contribute to the care a healthcare organization can provide. But often we need to start by assessing the mindset of the people providing that service.

Around 2011, the Air Force assigned me to lead a particularly challenging team in a military ambulatory medical center on the west coast of the United States. It was a stateside position; meaning we were dealing with day-to-day work on a typical base, typically undramatic and quite routine. When I moved into the flight commander position, there were a number of personality conflicts within the section. Multiple members did not enjoy working together, bad attitudes permeated the team, and trivial inconveniences or miscommunications would derail any positive tones between members.

After a few weeks, I reviewed our required inspection items and gleaned that the requirements of the day-to-day and annual operations were being met; from a formal standpoint, the section was performing above average as a unit.

Of course there were efficiencies or initiatives I could focus on improving. However, I also knew I would be working in the position for only a year or less due to scheduled military base moves.

So as I worked through my leadership goals for the position, I clearly evaluated:

- How I could positively affect the team
- What would be the greatest change in six to 12 months for these 25 people and the clinic we served
- Whether I should work on a more streamlined supply process or a team that supported each other, communicated well, put their teammates before themselves, and focused on the needs of the customer

I chose to focus on the latter. This team needed to shift their focus to serving others, including their own teammates. The core values of the U.S. Air Force are "Integrity First, Service Before Self, and Excellence in All We Do." Service is already at the forefront of the larger organization's overarching mission. Walking in uniform outside of the military base, I was frequently approached by strangers who said, "Thank you for your service."

However, when you are in the day-to-day grind of an office or clinical environment, it is easy to let the inconveniences or annoyances of serving your customers (internal or external) distract you from why you are there – to serve.

Realigning team priorities around service makes the focus customer-centric. I framed every conversation about what we needed to accomplish – personal and team goals – through the lens of service.

We worked together to identify opportunities to better our internal and external customer service. We focused our interactions between each other through the perspective of service – how can I make this person's day better? How can I help them meet their requirements and goals?

One of my favorite quotes from Mahatma Gandhi regarding service is, "The best way to find yourself is to lose yourself in the service of others." We adopted this philosophy within our team.

The office started to run more smoothly. Individuals started to help one another and conflict eased as general morale increased. We even picked a community service project that, as a team, we started working on together. It involved monthly trips to feed and serve the homeless on skid row in Los Angeles. We started within our team and quickly expanded it to employees throughout the whole clinic and military base. We focused on our clinical job *and* serving others outside of our organization.

Shifting the team's perspective to serving each other, other clinic employees, and our customers took time.

The perspective did not always stick with all team members or for every engagement, but it did make a difference in their work experience that year. I would hear team members reminding each other of our goal and mission of service. We created a culture of service – one interaction at a time.

It's the little things that make (or break) the customer experience
By Kelsey

Steve Jobs said, "You've got to start with the customer experience and work back toward technology – not the other way around." This application applies to technology and process. Any business touchpoint creates a customer experience.

In healthcare, patients are your most valuable, verbal, expectant, and vulnerable customers. Their customer experience influences their health – the most important aspect of life. After all, health usually dictates how long and engaged that life gets to be. Striving to make every patient experience the best customer experience must be a priority for every member of a healthcare organization. Improve the ~~hospital, waiting room, patient room, call center~~ experience.

As previously mentioned, my infant son was unexpectedly hospitalized in 2016. I had the unfortunate opportunity to spend a week in a children's hospital as a patient's mom instead of a consultant, partner, or employee.

Out of shear necessity (often related to infection control), certain aspects of hospitals cannot be changed. Does innovation happen to better healthcare and patient experience? Absolutely! But healthcare advances involve many more layers of consideration than other industries. For example, waiting rooms and patient rooms need to be able to be sanitized, so facilities have to pick furniture with that requirement in mind.

If you have ever spent a night (or in my case, six nights) as a guest in a patient room, you know that the convertible couches may be a necessity for practical space and cleaning reasons but are not a nice sleeping experience. During our stay, the nurses explained that the new children's hospital opening in 10 months would include regular beds for parents of patients (in the patient rooms!) and acknowledged the less-than-ideal sleeping arrangements my husband and I endured.

Our care team could not speed up the completion of the hospital to provide us with a real bed during our stay, but they did a number of things that I will remember far more than the uncomfortable convertible couch:

- Our nurse, Heidi, dropped off a few coupons for a 15-minute chair massage at two of the massage locations within the hospital. Then she checked in after a day or two to make sure we were using them and gave us more.
- They ensured we always had free parking coupons for ourselves and any visitors we had throughout our stay.
- When they would come in to check vitals on our son, they would take a few extra minutes to refill our water bottles with ice and water if they noticed they were empty on the nightstand.
- As one nurse was going on a break, she walked me to the hospital coffee shop so I found it right away.

There are big elements that structure a patient experience, but the little things that refine the engagement often make the most lasting impressions.

Decisions should benefit the end user
By Christoph

There's way too much talk about converting people to do what we want them to do.

It's about me, me, me – the organization who happens to own the website I'm on or whose social media account showed up in my feed while I was paying attention.

We focus on what we talk about. So if all we talk about is converting people by getting them to click on one thing or another, or if we only count engagement when they send money at the same time, that's what our decisions will be based on. We focus on those things over actually making an impression on people.

One of my favorite examples is enewsletter sign-ups that make me hand over my home address. Are they going to mail me a copy of the email newsletter? Nope. They want that to send me ads in the mail.

There are plenty of cases out there where decisions are made that benefit only the organization and not most users. A couple of examples include websites designed by committee and stories that are written to appease bosses but aren't relevant to external audiences.

Every time we create content online or add a feature to our website, we should ask ourselves how it helps our interested communities (target audiences).

Yes, yes, we feel like we have to think about the organization first. But when you put the consumer first, your organization will end up ahead of other organizations that follow common but terrible practices.

Every time we make a decision that doesn't benefit the end user it ultimately will hurt us, even if it works short-term. You don't want to beat the end user. You want to beat your competition.

I can't keep track of all the calls-to-action I'm supposed to follow. Everyone wants us to do something:

- Click here
- Buy this now
- Open my email, please
- Follow me on 59 other social media networks

I get it. Our livelihoods might depend on it. Success – even in content marketing and storytelling – is measured in dollars. Sometimes it takes a while for those dollars to come in, so it can be easy to declare strategies unsuccessful when they don't produce results on day two or three.

People buy from us when they know we are the best qualified organization or person to help with a particular problem. Sometimes it takes time for them to make a decision. Sometimes they don't have a need for the product at all.

A lot of times, the call-to-action is too early. When every blog post has a call to action to buy the same product, people will just tune that out – probably after seeing it less than a handful times. And duplicate calls-to-action are just as bad as irrelevant calls-to-action.

So how do we decide when to include a call-to-action? Here's my suggestion: If it benefits the user, add one. If it doesn't or it's self-serving, don't.

Some companies delight customers
By Christoph

It drives me crazy when I'm calling a company and get transferred and transferred and transferred. "Sorry, somebody else is in charge of that." Every transfer usually means I have to repeat my request, restate my password, my name, remember where my wife and I met, etc. Come on, people. This is not customer service. It's a game of keeping the customer away from more important things.

So when companies break this terrible mode of operation, it's a customer delighter that gets noticed. I recently noticed one when an online transaction inside the American Airlines app didn't go through. I called them and the first or second person took all the details of my request: My upgrade request didn't go through because of an outdated credit card on file, and they would have to transfer me to fix it. Ugh. This could take a while.

The next person quickly said, "One moment, Mr. Trappe. Let me just review my colleague's notes."

Even though that took a few seconds, it was so much more pleasant than me having to repeat my request, which is how some companies handle this kind of thing. The second person was caught up with the notes, had the right skills or access or whatever, and took care of everything. #Done.

Another delighter is calling a customer when they don't expect it. I ordered Charlotte Hornets tickets and a parking pass on StubHub. The parking pass couldn't be downloaded for a couple more days. When it was ready, StubHub called to let me know it was ready for download. What a delighter. How many internet-based companies call? I don't even like unscheduled phone calls in general, but I appreciated this one.

Another delighter: I dislike traveling late at night. I usually try to fly during the day or early morning so I can get to my destination at a reasonable hour. I need my beauty sleep. LOL. But sometimes there's just no way around flying late. That was the case when I arrived at Washington Dulles International Airport in October 2016. Wheels down around 11 p.m., and I still had a bit to go to the hotel.

The last thing I wanted was to deal with no rental car, an incorrect hotel reservation, or anything that would extend my day further. So I appreciated when everything went according to plan and then some.

As soon as we landed at Dulles, I received a text from Hertz, the car rental company I usually use, to let me know what stall my car was in. To get these texts, you have to sign up for free Gold service. This also allows you to skip the car rental lines. Hertz also offers the option to upgrade via text. Since one upgrade was free, I did it. "All set. We'll send you an updated carfirmation (which is what they call the text)."

When I got to the stall, the car's trunk was open, like somebody was saying, "We've been expecting you. Throw your luggage in here, and you are set to go." It was even more impressive since I had changed cars from the plane just moments earlier. Nonetheless, it was a delightful moment I appreciated.

As we move forward in automating as many processes as possible, we also need to remember to keep the human touch – or at least the perception of it. That's what delights customers. I have no idea if a Hertz employee manually opened that trunk (which I assume) or if it's some kind of computer script or something. "Customer changes car via text. Open trunk." I assume it was a human action, but even if it wasn't, it felt like one.

Some things to keep in mind as we continue to look for ways to delight our customers:

- Be nice. Always.
- Do what's unexpected – as long as it benefits the customer.
- Be super helpful.
- Never hide behind rules. Find a way to help.
- Sometimes we have to call for help.

Delighting customers can be hard because sometimes we have to "break process," and you know process is the most important thing to some people. It's understandable to a degree, because breaking some processes can have the opposite effect on customers. Think about a sandwich shop and an employee who is not making a sandwich according to the process. I wouldn't want that. Probably. I want the sandwich to my expectations or better. So if it's a better sandwich because they broke process, sure, I'm fine with that. But there may be some professional danger for that employee.

When delighting customers is done well, brand storytelling can happen at its finest. Customers will share your stories with their online and offline networks – these stories are most powerful when shared by others. Then you can reshare and respond to them. But first, the experiences have to happen. Be sure to create them for your customers.

And sometimes saying the obvious is customer-centric:

One Saturday, I needed to get some checks deposited and needed to find out how long the bank was open that day. The bank's website had all the information, and it was easy to find. The hours and location page also mentioned this: Online branch – always open.

Well, duh, of course online banking is always open – at least until a site is down for one reason or another. Why do we need to even mention it?

But thinking about it some more, it's brilliant to call out the obvious. It made me think about online banking and how, in theory, it can make things even easier. If I didn't already do online banking, it also might have caused me to look further into the service.

It was a good reminder that sometimes the obvious needs to be stated. It can help our customers. Sometimes incorrect information can cause you to lose customers

It was a long weekend in the United States with Independence Day 2016 on a Monday. Some businesses adjusted their hours to allow employees to spend a bit more time away from work. Good for them, but it's important to let customers know about that change.

Here's how my related experience unfolded. I asked my wife to see how long my typical dry cleaner would be open on the Saturday before the holiday.

"For another hour," she said, looking at their website, which had their hours listed. "We can make that."

When we got to the store, however, a sign taped to the door said they were closed for the holiday weekend. Good for them, but why not update the website?

So we carried on with other things, and I ended up going to a grocery store later in the day to mail out some copies of my book. I remembered that the store also has dry cleaning, though I had never used them. Why not try it since that dirty laundry was still in my car?

I dropped it off and gave them my business, in part because of the unnecessary experience earlier. I never would have put the laundry in the car had I thought they were closed.

Updating our websites should stay top of mind. It helps us get and keep customers, especially when we need to alert them of irregularities in hours, services, or anything that affects them.

Some organizations post these kinds of things on Facebook, Twitter, etc., and that's a good start, but not all customers will see them there.

It's important to align all channels to tell the same story, from your front desk team to your website and social media presence. Remember that operational changes impact customers, so keeping our websites updated along with other communication channels is important in creating a great customer experience.

Context and perspective: just another tumor, cancer, gunshot wound …
By Kelsey

I have a brain tumor.

In 2012, I was having some odd symptoms (TMI warning, but this is a piece on healthcare: galactorrhea to be exact). I Googled it and the results came back that I likely had a pituitary adenoma, a tumor on my pituitary gland. To the lay person, that means a brain tumor or breast cancer.

I was worried, and immediately scheduled an appointment with my primary care provider (PCP). The doctor explained that they would know much more once they took some blood tests. About two days later, I received an email that my test results were back. I hadn't yet heard from the doctor, so I logged on to my electronic medical record and saw that my prolactin levels were 40 times the normal limit. Meaning, I had a tumor on my pituitary gland.

I had a brain tumor. I was terrified. No one had explained what this meant. I Googled it again and remember reading about the side effects, including loss of vision and infertility, and that brain surgery may be necessary.

The next day I heard from my PCP. She couldn't tell me much more than that she was referring me to an endocrinologist, and that more tests would be necessary, likely fluid, blood, and an MRI of my brain.

I found out that I had a brain tumor through an electronic medical record alert. This is the wrong way to communicate with patients.

In the end, after three weeks of intense stress and worry, an easy-mannered and thorough endocrinologist explained that the MRI results showed a small-ish micro adenoma that was treatable with medication. He told me that I likely never would need surgery and that there were established treatments available to ensure my condition wouldn't interfere with starting a family someday.

The doctor explained all of the test results and how they molded his recommended course of treatment. He took a copious amount of time to answer my pre-prepared questions (thanks to weeks of Googling). He did this both in person during our initial visit and when he called me to explain the MRI results before they were available through my electronic medical record.

The manner in which we treat our patients should be the way we would want our family, unconnected to medicine, to be ushered through the system – gently, thoughtfully, thoroughly.

But how does a doctor think? In my own experience, I have noticed a disparity between the patient's expectation of urgency and the staff's sense of urgency with respect to the delivery of test results and the communication of care plans.

I recently asked my husband and some of his medical school classmates about their experiences training to be doctors. Many said they were initially surprised at the straightforward, scientific approach, especially of providers like surgeons or oncologists, when delivering test results.

On a surgery rotation, for example, one of them shared that they were surprised by how unemotional the providers were when dealing with Stage 1 cancer. It was a standard diagnosis, something that is common, treatable, straightforward, "no big deal." I don't want to call it nonchalance because they responded promptly to test results, informed the patient, and established thorough plans of care. It is hard for the provider and medical team to maintain a perspective of each patient's experience as they go from delivering a dire, Stage 4 cancer diagnosis to one patient, then delivering a Stage 1, completely treatable diagnosis to a patient in the next room.

But to the patient, any form of cancer diagnosis is cancer. Stage 1 or Stage 4, it is serious to them, it is stressful, and until they have had that thorough conversation about their plan of care with their provider, they likely don't understand the difference.

We cannot forget the importance of context. In 2014, my father was diagnosed with Stage 4 bone cancer. I thought it was a death sentence. I thought he would never get to meet his first grandchild ("in the oven" at the time). Then he met with his oncologist who explained that his type of cancer had a 50 percent remission rate. In 2015, he was in remission.

Working in hospitals, I remember friends coming to me to ask questions about getting appointments or about processing referrals. At the time, I thought I was helping them in whatever way I could as an added touch to their customer service. Looking back now, it should have been a red flag. They couldn't navigate the bureaucratic system easily as a patient on their own, or in a way that was convenient or effective. I was a staff member at the hospital and sometimes had a hard time getting responsive care (and I knew the staff really well!). I missed an opportunity for improvement.

When I received the automated email alert that my lab results were available, I was frustrated with my PCP for not taking the time to call me with my test results before I got them online. However, looking back, she was seeing 30 to 40 patients a day with too few nursing staff, medical technicians, and support teams. She was doing her best, and the system was set up to alert me immediately. Telling her to call the patient right away would have been fixing the wrong problem. There should have been a rule that when abnormal results come back, the patient doesn't get the alert until the provider releases it after they call, or within two days.

Healthcare has to improve. Providers are busy. They are more underpaid and overworked every year.

The patient experience also has to get better. We have to leverage our technology to fix patient experience issues and refine our communication. But our perspective as healthcare staff has to remain focused on the patient and their experience.

As healthcare providers, consultants, and staff, we have to remember that we see the crazy injuries, diagnoses, cancers, etc., every day, but to our patients, their experience matters. It's important, and it can be scary. They need our attention, compassion, and expertise. We cannot whitewash the severity of patient experience because of the breadth of our own practice.

Let me share a connection to this concept I made during a bad day in a war zone. In 2013, I was in Afghanistan leading our patient administration department at one of the two highest acuity trauma centers in the country. About halfway through my deployment, we had an alert drop that a medical evacuation helicopter was coming in. I asked what the injuries were, and one of my airmen said, "Just three patients, GSWs (gunshot wounds) to the legs and arms. Nothing big yet today."

To us, multiple gunshot wounds were not anything big for an afternoon during the "fighting season" in the middle of a war full of improvised explosive devices, landmines, gun battles, plane crashes, and more.

We had seen such horrific injuries by that point in our deployment that a few patients with gunshot wounds to their extremities were what we would consider minimally injured.

But what we never forgot was, for those troops coming in on that helicopter, it was a bad, bad day. It was a day they would remember forever; they would be physically and mentally scarred, in pain, and dreading the diagnosis and fallout from their injuries. We never treated them as less severe, less urgent, or less important than our patients with horrific injuries. We steadfastly maintained the same urgency and created the same level of customer experience through our care, service, communication, and reassurance.

All patients need that kind of commitment to urgency, transparency, thoroughness, and thoughtfulness. They do not see brain tumors, Stage 1 cancers, or gunshot wounds every day.

Many healthcare experiences are a scary time for patients, and our communication and treatment of them throughout their experience will set the context of their care and their experience with us. We have to use our knowledge, skills, and technology to make their experiences positive.

After all, we have the power to create an environment of thoughtful communication and treatment. The patient is vulnerable while we work – so, let's get it right.

Know your purpose
By Kelsey

Working in marketing, we easily can be sucked into pandering to stakeholders who are worried primarily about the bottom line. The bottom line is important. Isn't that what we're working for? Meeting our annual goals and hitting the highest ROI for our campaign budget? Or is it?

If Disney's purpose was to sell the most tickets and Mickey Mouse hats, would they be the massive marketing success they are today? No chance.

Instead, Disney is consistently exalted in business and marketing case studies because they know their purpose. They adjust how they communicate to customers based on their purpose. Disney describes their parks and resorts as "one of the world's leading providers of family travel and leisure experiences, giving millions of guests each year the chance to spend time with their families and friends, making memories that last a lifetime."

Their purpose is to create the opportunity for families to make memories. Do their ticket and Mickey Mouse hat sales contribute to their bottom line? Absolutely. But their purpose makes the customer relationship meaningful, sticky, and lasting. When every cast member interacts with families through this lens, they create a magical experience.

Are you creating a meaningful experience for your clients? Ask your organization: Why are we doing this [campaign, enewsletter, blog, promotion] again?

Remembering your purpose when working through a campaign strategy will significantly influence the success of the initiative.

I once heard a hospital CMO say that during every campaign strategy meeting, they wrote the word "patient" on a whiteboard in the room. Whenever they were making decisions or getting off track, anyone in the room could point to the board and remind the group who they were serving.

These campaigns drove business for their large hospital system. They brought more new patients into their organization for what they hoped would be long-term relationships, in turn generating millions of dollars annually. As the team executed their campaigns, they were perpetually mindful of their purpose: serving their patients.

That meant delivering premier customer service even at the "expense" of being "inconvenienced." In other words, doing something extra to serve the customer even though it might not be the easiest approach.

For example, they:

- Created easy online campaign conversions (even though it took more time to export the list and call patients back).
- Trained more team members to answer campaign calls so patients could book over the phone (even though the training required a bit more time).
- Did warm transfers every time (even though it's not the easiest way to transfer a call).
- Followed up with patients who converted at the initial part of the campaign to see how they could have improved their experience (even though the team had to create, distribute, and analyze the surveys and implement improvement initiatives).

In turn, their campaigns were consistently a smashing successes – creating long-term relationships while satisfying even the most jilted stakeholders who were focused on the bottom-line.

Now do it – make a difference. Know your purpose. Make sure your team knows your purpose. Use it to make customers want to continue the relationship because everything you do is about serving them.

Be transparent with your customers
By Kelsey

It will hurt your reputation if you don't keep the best interest of the customer in mind.

In May 2016, I was in Colorado for a wedding and talking to a personal and professional mentor of mine, Glenn Strebe. He is the CEO of a large and very successful credit union in Colorado, and he knows a thing or two about customer service.

We started talking about my blog and my motivation behind writing. He mentioned that over the years he has created training videos for his employees, and many of the videos focus on customer service. One of the stories he likes to tell to drive home the customer experience mentality goes something like this:

"You are on a long bike ride (Glenn has completed six Ironman triathlons, so he understands "long" rides!), and you stop at a gas station to get a Coke. Since you have been training so long, this is actually a good dietary option! You see the sign for a 32-ounce for $1.50 and fill up at the soda fountain, pay the cashier, and walk outside. After drinking your drink, you realize you need a bit more. Maybe 10 ounces or so will hit the spot. When you go back in to buy another refill, you see a sign you missed the first time: NEW Big Gulp, 45 ounces, 99 cents, limited time!

You think, 'Why wouldn't the cashier have let me know that the larger size was cheaper when he watched me pick out my size?' If you had known, you would have bought the larger size in the first place and would not have to go back in to pay more."

Christoph told me a related story when he was buying two Red Bulls he thought were on sale at a convenience store. The discount promotion was right in front of the cashier, but the discount didn't ring up. The cashier said the discount was for other sizes. Sizes that were about 2 ounces smaller and to the right of the sign. Annoying. The cashier ended up giving him the discount, but the signs were gone when he visited the next day. It was easier for the store to remove the discount than to adjust how it was promoted.

These kinds of experiences are frustrating. When a customer doesn't trust that a company has their best interest at heart, they won't trust them with their business long term.

For me, it's also an integrity issue – I don't want to feel "tricked" by a company because I didn't know the options available. Don't penalize me for not knowing what I don't know.

Now, pricing can be different across industries based on goods and services delivered. But if a customer is asking for something or expressing interest in a service, you always should share the best options so they know what choices they have. If you are not transparent with your customers, that's just bad customer service.

In 2015 my husband surprised me with a new purse. A friend expressed interest in buying one the following month, so I went online to share the link to the style I have. However, when I logged on to the site to find the purse, it was located in two places with two different prices – one was in the regular handbag section, and the second was in the sale handbag section.

I was a bit torqued. It felt like someone was trying to trick me. Was their mantra, "If customers don't check the sale section, they're going to pay full price?" In the existing website structure, the customer could not easily see that that the same bag was available for at least $120 less if you choose a different color. In this case, if you prefer dark pink you could save, but you have to find it in a different section first.

Maybe the website's information architecture needs to be reworked, or they should add a "you also may be interested in…" section that includes sale items related to those available at full price. Maybe it wasn't intentional.

Either way, in my experience, it felt bad. It felt like I was being tricked, but I caught on just in time to help my friend save money.

As organizations, we are responsible to ensure our customers know their options and that our recommendations are in their best interests.

Be transparent with your customers, build trust, and they will become loyal advocates. Be consumer-centric. Act in your customers' best interests – an authentic, focused, customer-oriented mindset is just good business.

People Need to Be Customer-Centric

Being nice
By Christoph

To be customer-centric in reality, you'll need more than the wish to be or the plan to do it. You'll need people who actually can implement it. That starts from the top down and carries all the way through to everyone on the front lines.

You'll need a visionary who makes it a priority, an implementer who comes up with the plan and processes. Sometimes good customer service falls down because processes handcuff employees. "Sorry, I can't do that because this system literally doesn't let me." But let's not overthink processes. To offer good customer service aside from the technical side of things (think the purses) is a mindset. Decide to offer good customer service. Go! Repeat.

To provide great customer service, the people who are communicating with the customers have to be able to do two things:

- Know what they're talking about and what customers need
- Be nice

Of course, the company also must empower them to be helpful, but those are two things employees can control themselves.

Even if employees are hired in a field that is new to them, they can learn about the products, the mission, and everything else to provide customer-centric service. The best of the best seek out information. Yup, companies offer training programs, and some of it is better than others, but these employees don't just take on a victim mentality when training is bad or unclear. They want to learn more and they do. Their interest and drive for more information ultimately helps their customers later on.

The best customer-centric people also are nice. They don't yell. They don't put people off. They find solutions. They know the rules well enough to figure out how to work within them to get things done. They know the importance of smiling when a distressed customer needs something. They also know the importance of speedy responses. On social medial, responding quickly is especially important, but let's not forget about offline – where most of our lives happen.

Some people have natural tendencies to be nicer than others. How do we find them and hire them for our organizations? Here are some ideas:

- Make it crystal clear in the job description that being nice is part of the culture – internally and externally. Being nice doesn't mean being a pushover or never disagreeing. It means being pleasant and helpful.
- Ask potential team members how they've worked through stressful situations. You'll want the person who can stay calm and helpful, but also can be firm when things are stressful.
- Check their social media profiles. If they're public, they're fair game. It's hard to see somebody being nice if they aren't very nice on Twitter.
- Ask about their general outlook on life. People with a positive, non-arrogant outlook and attitude may be more suited for being nice.
- Find out if helping people comes naturally to them. If something happens while they're waiting, for example, do they jump in to help?

Not everyone out there is nice or even wants to be. And it can come down to the stories we tell ourselves and the ones our communities play back to us. If everyone has a bad attitude, it's easy to also have a bad attitude. When we make a point to be nice, friendly, and helpful, others will follow.

Of course, just being nice isn't enough. At the end of the day, customers want help getting some kind of problem fixed. So if companies have too many restrictive policies that prohibit nice employees from actually helping customers, that won't be enough, either. Hire nice people who know what they're talking about, and give them the authority to help customers.

Digital strategists can be customer advocates
By Christoph

Digital strategists can be great customer advocates. They help organizations define how digital experiences are shaped. That often means what goes on a website, how easy is it for people to do certain things, and how it all integrates with the overall experience.

There are three big camps of digital strategists:

- Those who talk
- Those who know
- Those who dump data

The talkers

The first group sounds really good – you know when they're talking. They throw around the latest buzzwords. They tell you it's about engagement, calls to action, blah blah blah. They even say it's about storytelling, but they aren't talking about what we're talking about – actual strategy. They just know it's a buzzword, and the rule is to use the latest buzzwords. As often as possible. With and without context.

They talk circles around you so quickly that their stuff sounds reasonable.

The knowers

And then there's the second big camp, which is the people who know. Now, they sometimes are good talkers, but unlike the first group, they have data to back things up.

As Kelsey mentioned, website expert Andy Crestodina has warned to not bring "an opinion to a data fight." One of my favorite quotes, for sure. The knowers don't bring opinions. They bring facts based on data gathered from user behavior. Then they make decisions based on these facts.

Knowers don't guess. They don't make up stuff. They know what works and are honest enough to admit that a 5 percent click through rate in an email newsletter is not something to write home about, for example.

And here's the thing. Even though they know, they also change their opinions and knowledge when user behavior changes and data supports it.

As much as the talkers might be entertaining to listen to, I would recommend listening to the knowers. The hard part is to figure out which group somebody fits into. Here's a hint: Knowers have relevant data.

The data dumpers

Then there are the data dumpers. Now, I've known rock star data analysts who can tell you what the numbers mean and help you improve based on what they're seeing. That's not who we're talking about here. The data dumpers just drop numbers in front of you and claim it's an analysis.

Sometimes they see a spike and claim they've discovered something. A spike! LOL. I can see it, too. But unless we can explain it, it's not analysis.

Don't mistake data dumpers for knowers. Look at the data, make decisions on content constantly, and be flexible to change on a moment's notice to test if theories are right. Then keep producing authentic stories and keep testing.

The content production/testing loop never stops. The only stop is irrelevance, and we don't want to stop there.

What makes a great digital strategist? Digital strategists can work closely and successfully with authentic storytellers (content marketers). The best digital strategists understand this and help us rebuild the airplane while we are flying it. On the other hand, the two disciplines also can butt heads and waste time with unnecessary power struggles.

Authentic storytellers often are – or should be – good at finding ways to get great stories published in the most efficient and meaningful way.

Yes, there are strategic ways and times to release stories. Really, for the most part, those "strategic" moves are overthought and when they don't work, those same planners try to analyze why and forget about publishing more great stories.

For the most part, if we have a great story, we should publish it now or make sure it gets on the regular schedule. It works. I've seen it in every project that follows my authentic storytelling process. I still maintain that blogging at least once a week at the same time is the way to go. From there, content should be distributed on at least five more channels. Sharing our stories – especially those that highlight great customer service and when we learned how to improve it – can actually help us as a company become more customer-focused.

The key is to keep things moving and keep sharing those stories in line with our goal of helping customers.

Plans are great, but plans with phased functionality are best. It used to be that projects were run like this: Make a plan that includes every single detail. Once every detail was ironed out, the implementation would start. Or, so much time would pass that there would be enough turnover in the organization that a new plan had to be started. And then when the project launched, that was that. On to the next project.

Today, things move way too fast in the digital space to plan and write plans months at a time. There needs to be movement.

Get the minimally working product to market and update it from there based on changes in the marketplace and in user behavior. Sometimes we can even uncover user behavior that we previously overlooked.

This also applies to launching content marketing and authentic storytelling strategies. Start being nice and then start gathering and writing stories. Pieces of them can be shared on social media right now. The full stories can be shared on the blog when it's live.

Many software applications that are part of our lives use this approach, too. Think of all the devices that have regular software upgrades. Same thing.

Phased functionality can help us get to market faster and make updates and adjustments live. When done right, it benefits the organization and the consumer.

In content marketing, things change quickly. Yesterday's Facebook strategy may not work tomorrow because Facebook changed something. They can do that, and as much as some people complain, most of us have no vote and must adjust our own strategies.

The problem with an ever-changing digital landscape is that things need to get done quickly, while the long-term plan is kept in mind and also moved forward.

The best digital strategists handle these two seemingly conflicting pieces with ease. They also look at common practices and don't mistake them for best practices – even when other experts call them that.

As I said before, when we copy other people's crap, we just produce more crap.

Leadership focus: Help customers convert more, work less, and enjoy the experience
By Kelsey

Don't make customers work to give you their business. And while they're interacting with you, make it easy (and fun) to be your customer. Having organizational leaders who espouse this thinking will align your team with customer-centricity.

Business occurs when a customer converts. They go from being a prospect to being your customer. Conversions happen in person, over the phone, or on your website. Similar principles apply to all customer touchpoints. As we walk through a few recommendations, you will see how they permeate all customer experiences, regardless of the medium.

In person or over the phone, personal interactions (or call routing) usually differentiate an experience. A customer service representative can make a conversion easy, pleasant, hard, or nearly impossible for a customer.

Online, thinking through the information architecture, web design elements, and usability can help ease the user experience throughout your site. Amazon does this well with the "1-click to buy" feature for Amazon Prime members, a simple checkout, and so helpfully recommending things I may also be interested in based on past purchases.

But so often, companies make customers work. This boggles my mind – companies want business, yet still get stuck doing business in a way that's easiest for them, not best for the customer. Companies make customers work to find the right phone number online or the right hours so they can bring in business.

One evening, my husband and I were enjoying a rare, childless date night and planned to try a sushi restaurant a friend had recommended. First, we could not find them in Google to get the directions for almost five minutes (a near eternity for two web-savvy searchers). Once we did, their hours were listed as closed (it was Sunday around 4 p.m.), and the listed phone number was no longer in service. We went somewhere else only to found out later that the restaurant actually was open that afternoon. I have since heard from two more friends that the restaurant has great food and efficient service, but if a new customer has to work so hard to get in the door, it's not a great experience. We still haven't tried the restaurant.

Customers have so many options in today's markets. They really don't need to interact with you, and there is always an alternative. So give them reasons to easily convert, and while you're at it, make it a nice experience that builds long-term loyalty.

Here are four ideas for how to foster customer-centric experiences:

1. **Convenience, convenience, convenience**

When I managed a group practice for a military ambulatory clinic, one of our KPIs was flu shot compliance. In the military, patient health correlates to operational readiness. We had open walk-in times for our three-week fall immunization push, and compliance rates were low every year.

The second year, we took the flu shots to the patients. We had the luxury of knowing where the majority of our patients worked – it was a military base after all! So for those three weeks, we rotated through office buildings, logistic shops, the fitness center, and command offices giving flu shots. When lines slowed down in the designated room within those buildings, we walked the halls, knocked on offices, and brought the flu shots to our patients.

Today's patients expect accessible care within their schedule – telemedicine couldn't be more timely. Remote provider visits, or virtual visits, through easy applications, are changing the way patients approach care for common aliments like a cold, sinus infection, or UTI.

Outside of healthcare, apps like OrderUp make meal delivery available, easy, and fast. Or if you'd prefer to cook for yourself, Blue Apron or Hello Fresh will send you prepackaged ingredients. Or, if you want to pick out ingredients yourself, many grocery stores now offer shopping online and free delivery. Companies stand out when they make the customer experience convenient.

2. Easy to find, easy to convert

Can your customers even find you? I started working with a hospital more than three years ago, and I Googled medical services in their area – they were nowhere. Well, page six-plus in Google can sometimes be the equivalent of nowhere.

Have you done any mystery shopping within your own organization? I don't mean calling a call center and asking a question about hours of operation. I mean putting yourself in your customers' shoes with a real goal in mind, and experiencing the path they take within your organization to convert. Developing personas can help you identify these key audiences and formulate scenarios to help improve their experience.

Still having a hard time identifying barriers to service or conversion? Ask your customers and your staff. I have had some of the most insightful conversations with call center attendants, front desk clerks, and information desk staff. They know the pain points to the customer experience, and once the issues are identified, many are easily resolved.

3. Clear expectations

Years ago, one of my mentors said, "I will always be very clear with you, because when we have clear expectations, we're less likely to be disappointed." This is true as you lead your team, and it also applies to every customer touchpoint.

In 2015, I remember calling my contracted insurance provider for maternity benefits after I had my son. I was cut off and transferred three times before getting to the right person. It was annoying to be mid-sentence explaining what I thought I needed only to be transferred without warning. The first time I thought the call dropped!

However, I love calling my son's pediatrician's office at the University of Iowa Hospitals and Clinics. When I talk to operators, they appropriately route me to a scheduler or the nurse on staff. They tell me exactly what they are going to do and what to expect before I am transferred. If I share any information with them, they pass it along.

I don't repeat myself, it's efficient, it's a friendly experience, and it's easy to give them my business. An extra bonus: I don't sit through three minutes of "press 1 for scheduling, press 2 for the pharmacy, press 3 for our front desk …" with my fingers crossed that I pick the right one and don't have to redo the horrible recording.

4. Make it fun:

One of my favorite videos adeptly demonstrates how making something fun can influence behavior. It's by The Fun Theory, a 2009 initiative of Volkswagen.

In the video, the question is posed, "Can we get more people to choose the stairs by making it fun to do?" By turning the stairs into a staircase-size piano, they did just that – 66 percent more people took the stairs over the neighboring escalator.

Does your company make it fun to be a customer? When my son was hospitalized in 2016, I was walking to the cafeteria one afternoon and there was a steel drum band playing. It was a light moment during a scary week.

I recently saw a picture on Twitter that was shared by a parent whose child was being treated for a broken wrist at Children's Hospital of Wisconsin. The hospital gave him a shirt that said, "I did it for the cool cast." They put red and yellow colors over his cast since his arm is "under construction." Now that makes being a customer more fun, even in a less-than-ideal situation.

Convenience, easy interactions, clear expectations, and a fun experience makes great customer interactions.

Making things easy should be easy
Christoph

On the topic, of making things easy, I'm reminded of an interaction I had with my internet provider.

We cut satellite TV and added some much cheaper internet TV stations. Since there are more than 10 different devices connected to our Wi-Fi, the internet stations were kind of slow. I went to my internet provider's website, ready to order a faster package.

It turns out that I couldn't do that. The internet provider doesn't offer online ordering. How about that! Their website told me to call them, which I did. Since it was the weekend, however, they were closed. The voicemail asked me to call back on Monday. Of course, by Monday I had forgotten about it and didn't follow through.

How do companies measure how much money they lose because of solutions that are not customer-centric?

Barriers to Being Customer-Centric

The pressure of perfection in social media
By Kelsey

Times have changed since the explosion of social media. Fifteen years ago, you knew when your high school or college reunions were looming and you could primp a polished-looking life to display. Now, you are "friends" with distant acquaintances who can peek into your life anytime you post online.

With the pressure to show the best version of yourself or your organization at all times, social media's insight into your "real" life gets more muddled while our perception of other people's lives drifts further and further from reality. That disparity between perception and reality creates disillusionment and unhappiness while incubating a bit of narcissism in us all. And how could it not? When you compare your real experiences with the polished reality others project as "real" online, disappointment is inevitable.

When my husband and I got married in 2010, Pinterest had just been established two months prior. It was still unknown as the go-to for wedding ideas. We had a few do-it-yourself elements like centerpieces, and I had no idea where to start. I bought a couple of wedding magazines and found a picture of some candles on a large plate with rose pedals, and we were done. It was basic – very basic.

Now, brides spend hours pinning, browsing, and sharing to collect perfect inspirations for every element of their wedding festivities. In 2013, the Huffington Post reported that a "whopping 91 percent of brides say they go online to search for wedding inspiration."[1]

Seeing everyone else's "Pinterest Perfect" wedding imagery raises their expectations, and arguably their displeasure when they can't quite meet the perceived standard of creativity, cuteness, and style.

All of the pressure to project a perfect social media presence that somehow translates to reality is ludicrous.

I have a lovely little boy. However, after he was born in 2015, I had to stay off of social media for a while because the perceived perfection made my reality seem dismal.

After about two weeks with my sweet, sleepy newborn, a screaming, colicky minion emerged. For more than three months he would scream and cry nearly

---

[1] http://www.huffingtonpost.com/2013/07/17/online-wedding-planning_n_3607416.html

inconsolably for hours and hours – many days totaling five or more hours of severe fussiness. At night, he didn't sleep more than a couple hours at a time. Bouncing, swaying, and walking (all in an exhaustingly timed combination) eased the screaming, but as soon as you stopped, sat down, or put him down, the hysterical screaming commenced again.

In my rare moments of peace, I browsed Facebook and it seemed like all I saw were smiling, sweet, cuddly, and sleeping babies. I'd expected to experience that calm during my precious few months of maternity leave. Instead, I was taking morning walks around a pond near our house while my newborn screamed for the full hour – taking a quick break only when I picked him up, bounced him, and dragged the stroller behind me.

So, about two months in, I posted a smiling image of my son. It was a day where I finally felt like I had a "normal" baby. A few expectedly fussy moments, but no hours of insanely irrational crying (although it did return the next day). When I posted this picture with the caption, "This little nugget is officially having the happiest day of his life ... I may pay for it tomorrow, but thank goodness colic is not forever ☺," I quickly received more than 140 likes and 20 comments. Between the comments and personal messages, eight people reached out to tell me they were either currently dealing with a colicky baby, or had experienced one. They offered encouragement and access if I wanted any tips. Most importantly, I realized that seeing the social media photos of friends' perfect babies doesn't mean they aren't going through the same crap. They just haven't chosen to share that part of their story.

If you share your story in a way that is more representative of reality, it is more powerful. You can inspire, console, entertain, and connect with other people. It doesn't have to be all good or all bad. Share both! Share the inspiring and, most importantly, share what is real.

In marketing, organizations are always trying to share inspiring stories. The Super Bowl in 2016 was packed with sentimental commercials. A State Farm commercial highlighted the values of family, showing both the good and bad moments of each stage of parenting.[2] It was cute. I remember it because I have had all of those moments, but it also was produced.

When an organization can translate the real story and share it through social media, it leaves a lasting impression because it is inspiring through the unveiled reality and vulnerability. My grandmother passed away in the summer of 2016 after a nearly 15-year battle with Parkinson's. It's a horrible disease I am unfortunately

---

[2] https://youtu.be/O1Z91YkPatw

too familiar with. One of the side effects is uncontrollable tremors.

In 2014, I first saw a video made by SCL Health System. I teared up when I saw it and heard a patient, Fred, describing the blessed effects of his surgery. An avid archer, his tremors had forced him to give up his hobby. However, after a brain implant to subdue the tremors, he describes the feeling of when he was first able to hold a pen and then pull a bow back without shaking. He said, "the tears just came down."

A few months ago, I was describing it during a talk I gave about telling impactful stories when connecting project impact with organizational results. Halfway through telling the story, I choked up and had to take a moment to collect myself. Years later, that video still elicits emotion – even just thinking about it now. My grandmother was forced to give up golf, bowling, and her daily walks to Catholic mass as her Parkinson's progressed and tremors got worse. Fred's story, through its authenticity, connects with a customer beyond a marketing message. It leaves a lasting impact on anyone who can connect to the reality, the transparency, and the genuineness of the experience it shares.

When we share real experiences on social media, we connect with others online in a more genuine way.

Comparing the pre-social media era to now, I argue that as people, we haven't really changed. We are still overly focused on "looking good." Fifteen years ago, it was contained to a new haircut, a diet, and a new outfit before a high school reunion full of small talk and photo sharing – in person. Now it's maintaining a hip, witty, picture-perfect online persona at all times.

Social media provides an avenue to maintain that glossy persona of an organization and the opportunity to be real and share honestly. The persona you portray in social media is up to you. The further you stray from the "Pinterest Perfect," Instagram-edited persona, the closer you are to reality. More often than not, I only remember the real experiences in my social media feeds – especially when they come from organizations who have shared reality.

Being real on social media creates moments of authentic connectivity with your customers. It offers a breath of genuine, fragrant air in the cloud of sterile social media perfection.

When creating a lovely customer experience leaves a bigger impact on you
By Kelsey

Religions regularly espouse the value of giving. In Christianity, especially around the holidays, you often hear, "it is more blessed to give than to receive" (Acts 20:35).

When you create a wonderful patient experience, you give that person something that is out of their control to influence. When you do this, you change their experience for the better. First, a little background …

During my time in the Air Force, I served as the director of patient administration for the largest level 1 trauma center in Afghanistan. I saw 888 trauma patients within my six-and-a-half-month deployment and thousands of non-critical outpatient and humanitarian patients. My team's main responsibilities included patient tracking, bed availability reporting, patient valuable inventory, patient weapon security, death processing, medical records, and patient registration.

This was an impactful year – it was the most meaningful work I have ever done, and it also taught me about the beauty of service.

The experiences I remember most revolve around opportunities to create a better experience for patients.

Unexpectedly, those patient experiences left a lasting impact on me.

I'll tell you about two of them. First, the hassle of an electronic medical records (EMR) system in a war zone. Again, a little background.

We had to enter all patients into our EMR system upon arrival so the providers could process orders. This meant that for outpatient visits, we registered everyone into an EMR through our office.

The military's "home grown" EMR system was a combination of an efficient but painfully inflexible DOS system, a 1990s paper-based medical records office, and an up-and-coming but not quite refined version of a web EMR program. Needless to say, it could be painful to use at times, for staff and patients.

When you think of a war zone hospital, you probably envision the treatment of battle injuries. Yes, we had many of those. I saw a lot of trauma. But thousands of our patients were for outpatient procedures or minor treatment – the common cold, flu, and appendicitis does happen in a war zone. Our family practice office frequently was packed with service members.

What many people do not realize is that we also conducted regular humanitarian appointments for local men, women, and children. There were two additional hospitals on our base – one run by the Egyptian military and one run by the equivalent of the South Korean Red Cross. These operated solely for humanitarian purposes, and they escalated their most complex cases to our team.

Since our EMR patient tracking was based off of a U.S. social security number, we had to create identification cards for these patients, many of whom were illiterate or could only provide one name. We had to add pseudo-social security numbers to be used for record tracking. This worked for the initial visit, but when people returned for follow-ups and did not bring their pseudo-numbers, or didn't spell their names the same way, we could not find the matching patient identifiers to give their records to the providers.

One day, a young Afghan girl was ushered in by the Egyptian medical representative. She was in a long, blue traditional firaq partug and headscarf. Based on her height, stature, and facial features, I would have guessed she was about 12 years old. She clutched a baby who looked about 10 months old, and who needed to see our neurosurgeon. When I asked the girl's name through the translator, she told the translator a first name. But he explained to me that she could not spell it, so he provided his best guess.

This was a common experience for young women about her age, as the Taliban had prohibited girls from attending school for the last 15-plus years. Every time I met one of these far-too-young child brides and illiterate young mothers, my heart sank. I couldn't change their circumstances, but I could give them a positive experience while they were in our hospital.

We provided her a patient identifier and the translator walked her to see the neurosurgeon who would be treating the baby. Within 15 minutes, I had a livid doctor, the Egyptian translator, and the mother and baby back in our office.

The doctor was frustrated that the young woman said she had seen the previous neurosurgeon for a procedure for the baby, but he could not find the record. Most doctors rotated every six to nine months. The girl did not understand anything that was previously done for the child.

I could tell that the doctor was incensed. Months of being sleep deprived, living in the dorms, being away from family, and seeing the kinds of patients we did was incredibly taxing on all of our team. I also could tell the mother was terrified.

We had to create a better experience for everyone involved. I asked the doctor to go back to his office, and we would do some research and bring all of the records we could find to him. I offered the mother some snacks (we always had a stockpile from care packages), and I asked someone on the team to bring the baby a toy, which we kept on hand for pediatric patients. Then the team began to scour our databases, looking for a matching diagnosis and similar name.

I remember this experience because there was nothing the girl could do – she was scared that her baby wouldn't get treatment. She was helpless, powerless, and intimidated, which the language barrier only exacerbated. We reassured her through the translator that we would find her information, but it may take a little while. We eventually did, and her baby was treated.

She may not remember my team, but she is a vivid memory for me. Creating that experience left a lasting impression because for that day, our work made a positive impact in her life.

Here's my second story, which is about a personal touch in the ER at the base.

My team was responsible for meeting trauma and emergency patients at the triage location, assisting in collecting their valuables, securing their weapons, annotating the initial diagnoses, and starting the patient tracking process. In the typical 72-hour whirlwind of treatment and transport back to the U.S., I would not expect any of those patients to remember interfacing with my team.

There was one incredibly busy day when we had over 15 patients coming in from an attack at a neighboring base. All were transported by helicopter in batches of two or three at a time. One of the last groups arrived later in the evening. Their injuries were the least severe of the day, mostly uncomplicated gunshot wounds to their extremities. But they also were the youngest troops of the day, ranging in age from 19 to 21.

I remember welcoming this group as they were brought into the emergency room. We delivered care packages of clean clothing and toiletries as we collected and verified their information.

Throughout the bustle in the room, a young marine looked up at me as I explained what was in his care package. He looked scared, tired, and a bit overwhelmed. I stopped, put my hand on his forearm, and said, "Welcome to Bagram. We have been waiting all day for you. We are going to take great care of you." He smiled and visibly relaxed into the stretcher.

Taking the time to welcome him brought a personal touch to the chaos of his patient experience. And he is one of my most vivid memories of that job, regardless of whether he remembers me.

Who benefits from the patient experience? Do patients remember their experiences years later? Maybe not, nor should we expect them to remember. However, taking the time to create positive experiences when patients are in need can leave a lasting impact on us.

Some audiences need different things
By Christoph

Some audiences want more details. Some just want the highlights, and others might want to ask follow-up questions. But if your customer care team is restricted to reading scripted responses, they won't always be nimble enough to make an interaction a conversation.

I'm frequently reminded of this when I keynote or give workshops. Different people have different needs and wants.

Here's an example. When I talk to groups about storytelling, content marketing, or social media, I share the importance of stories. To show the power of stories, I ask everyone to share one of their own. Usually, people start connecting and start friendly conversations. Stories are powerful and build relationships, after all.

At a presentation in May 2016, one of the male participants shared the story surrounding a child being born in his family. He shared how the baby's parents had tried for a while and finally were able to have a child. He even described in detail how he first met the new baby.

I told him, "Congratulations. Thank you for sharing." It was a great story and he certainly felt good about it. Others in the room were smiling. But were the details relevant for this group?

I turned to the rest of the group, many of whom were women, and asked, "Who here is wondering what the baby's gender is?" He didn't mention it, but of course, many in the group nodded yes.

"And who really wants to know the baby's weight and size?" Again, everyone.

Of course, he shared this information immediately. But why wasn't it shared in the first place? We discussed what had happened. Different people think about different details. Picking the right details to share with audiences can strengthen our connections.

As we share stories, it's important to remember our audience. Sometimes they want different details than those we might care about personally. Sometimes the audience might tell us what details they missed and want to hear, as was the case in my example. Many times, however, we won't get that feedback. When we do, following up can positively impact the relationship.

Scripts can hurt customer service
By Christoph

Using our own words in our own voice helps authenticity. Here's an example. I called customer support to get help with a product I was using at home.

The customer service rep who answered had a sense of humor and definitely did not stick with the company script. Now, that sometimes can cause problems, and us marketing folks might not appreciate that at first glance. There's a script for a reason, right?

But seriously, that's the easy answer. The message is spelled out, but can everyone read it in an authentic way?

This rep was caught off guard by my name. "Christian? No, Chris – what? Oh, Christoph. OK, I don't know a Christoph, just a Christian. But OK, how can I help you?"

Now, people have called me Chris or said things like, "Oh, is it supposed to be Christopher and they forgot the E-R on here?" This can be kind of annoying. But this guy pulled it off in a nice, conversational way. It helped his authenticity. Plus, I felt like his day may have been as long as mine had been. And who doesn't want to talk to a real human?

Once I told him my problem, he said, "Oh, that should be easy. People have been calling with much more difficult things all day."

At one point he was stumped. "Well, it says in here to do this, but that doesn't work for you?" I heard a groan. That probably wasn't scripted either, but I felt the same way!

It was Valentine's Day and he even shared a Valentine's Day story from the call center. It was kind of fun, and he built a connection and got the problem fixed. Perhaps just as important, the call wasn't frustrating!

This again reminds me that it's not important to memorize the talking points, or even read a script (unless you absolutely have to, and there might be times for that). The important things to remember are the company's mission, your tasks to achieve the mission, and figuring out ways to get there.

Bottom line: Being authentic while helping customers can build strong connections to your company's mission.

Communication is a huge reason why we might not be as customer-centric as we think. It's easy to miscommunicate. Even one-word sentences can lead to miscommunication. Here's an example.

I bought something at a store.

"Receipt?" the cashier asked.

"Yup."

"Okay, bye. Have a great day."

"Can I get my receipt?"

I guess my "yup" sounded like a "nope." Maybe I do pronounce my yeses in a no kind of way. Who knows.

But it's a good reminder how easy miscommunication actually is. People mishear things or mumble, and maybe we were thinking about something else while they were talking.

Think about more complicated discussions. Miscommunications will happen, guaranteed. Just work through them. Some ways to avoid miscommunication:

- Watch reactions. Do they align with the discussion?
- Ask, "Would you like me to go over it again?" if anyone seems unsure.
- Ask people to explain their understanding. Just make sure you don't come across as condescending.

Uncorrected miscommunications cause us to live and remember the wrong stories. Be sure to catch and correct miscommunications. It's the only way for people to remember and share the right stories.

Inconveniences are unavoidable: How you respond matters
By Kelsey

Some customer inconveniences are unavoidable. When those circumstances pop up, the way the organization responds leaves a lasting impression on customer experience.

During one of my first jobs as a hospital administrator, our organization started a major, 18-month construction project in a large ambulatory clinic. Patients used alternative entrances, and clinics relocated into smaller areas and spread out between multiple floors. Inconveniences abounded on every floor and within every area of the facility.

There wasn't anything that got easier for the patients during this time and, to be honest, we could have done a lot to create a smoother transition through the construction period. We didn't add any perks to ease the inconveniences – the organizational mentality was more like, "We're suffering through it right alongside you." That's not an effective approach to build customer satisfaction, loyalty, or advocacy.

When I went to visit a friend who had a baby at the University of Iowa Hospital in 2016, there was a large and beautiful care package in her hospital room. I commented on the lovely wrapping, and my husband, who had finished his OB/GYN rotation through labor and delivery a few months earlier, said that the boxes were from the construction company working on a renovation project adjacent to the mother-baby rooms. They had received complaints about the daytime noise from mothers recovering from delivery, and they'd responded with beautiful care packages.

Construction noise is unavoidable when an organization is going through a renovation. So the company could have shrugged off the complaints as expected or acceptable – instead they responded in a way that eased the inconvenience for the hospital's patients.

In the boxes, there was a note congratulating the new mother on her baby, acknowledging the noise, and promising to keep it down as much as possible. The box also included some treats to make their stay in the hospital a little sweeter: chocolate, caramel popcorn, a newborn swaddle sack, and a few other goodies.

Later that summer, I was at an art festival in the downtown area of my city. The city is transitioning one of the main streets into a walking street. Consequently, a large construction zone would block off much of the street for the next few months. Usually, these construction zones are quite an eye sore, especially for surrounding restaurants and shops that are trying to entice customers to sit outside and enjoy the sidewalk patios.

Instead, I turned the corner to the construction zone and saw hundreds of streamers flapping in the wind. They had provided stations for passers-by to cut and tie multi-colored ribbons around the chain linked fence. When viewed at an angle, as most people do as they walk along the sidewalk, it looked quite nice.

If you face the construction zone straight on, the fence doesn't completely block the unsightly view. But the decorations made the unavoidable inconvenience a little easier on the eyes.

Some customer inconveniences are unavoidable. As organizations focused on the customer experience, our job is to ease the annoyance of these inconveniences through alternatives or by making the inconvenient experience as nice as possible.

Apply empathy: It benefits your business and your customer

By Kelsey

Business leaders easily can get sucked into focusing on the bottom line and initiatives that enhance revenue. The most fiercely raging fires require your attention, and going from fire to fire quickly sucks up your time, energy, and influence, leaving little oomph for more intentional pursuits. But turn the table and ask, how often have you interacted with a company and felt like they were oblivious to the real people using their services or buying their products?

Businesses that lack empathy view customers as singular contributions to their bottom line instead of understanding them as actual people. They hold too rigidly to their policies. Using empathy would bend policies to better serve the customers.

In 2014, I was 7 and a half months pregnant. It was a Tuesday, and I received the horrific news that one of my dearest friends had lost a young family member unexpectedly. I booked a flight to attend the funeral – it was last minute, so I scheduled over the phone while sitting in a dark parking lot at the grocery store after work that evening. I didn't buy travel insurance like I usually did throughout my pregnancy – it wasn't offered by the clerk over the phone, and I didn't remember to ask.

The next morning, I had a routine OB appointment and was planning to fly out that evening to attend the funeral the following day. During the checkup, the baby's heart rate was diving and rising without the usual frequency. As my OB calmly explained to me, "It's okay for the heart rate to drop below the limits we like to see, but in your case, the baby's heart rate isn't recovering at the frequency we prefer." After an extra hour of monitoring in the office, they sent me to the hospital to be admitted for a longer period of monitoring. I would miss my trip. My heart lifted four hours later when they determined the baby was fine, then sank again with the realization that I would miss the opportunity to support my friend.

I went through the annoying steps of cancelling the trip I had scheduled the day before. After checking the website for additional information, I called the airline and was told a refund would not be an option, and there was nothing the representative could do.

The next day, I called to speak with a customer service representative after finding on the site that a hospitalization of the traveler is a refundable exception to their policy.

Over the next three weeks, I spoke with five representatives as I was bounced around different departments. I submitted two online refund request packages after I was provided incorrect information the first time. Then, after 21 business days, I received a denial of the refund in an email. I called once more and was told there was no appeal process.

I experienced an overwhelming feeling of powerlessness to communicate to this company, or rectify my situation. Then I (hormonally) processed the feeling of being wronged since my situation completely fell into the stipulations within their refund policy. It was infuriating.

I did not have a single interaction where I felt heard, understood, or cared for as an individual.

There was no empathy woven into their policy or customer interactions – and likely not because the individuals following their customer scripts didn't have empathy or understanding, but because the organization didn't prioritize the delegation of decision making to act in the interest of the customer.

Organizations have to care about their customers and clients enough to provide service representatives with the ability to "make the call" to shift the customer experience to the positive. To provide a refund, to comp a drink or meal, to fit in an extra doctor appointment at the end of a full schedule to accommodate a very sick child.

By relinquishing some of your corporate control and empowering your employees, you make your organization more powerful to influence the customer experience at every juncture. It provides your organization the opportunity to show empathy at the individual level, and your customers will remember that.

Corporate policies may be intended to be empathetic to the user, but more often they come across as rigid, bureaucratic edicts that can't flex based on individual situations.

How much would it have hurt that airline to allow their phone representatives to flex ticket refund requests like mine that exactly matched their online refund policy? Yes, probably some impact to the bottom line, but by doing so, they also would have the opportunity to gain a loyal customer. Instead, my premium status is now with a different airline carrier.

Automation and Technology: Customer-Centric or Not?

Automation isn't always good
By Christoph

I volunteered more than 100 hours in 2014, but unfortunately I had to cancel an assignment once in a while.

I had signed up to volunteer at a weekend event that fall. The week before, I received an automated email from the organizer reminding me of my assignment and where to go. Automation worked in this case. They spelled my name right, the email made sense, and I got the info I needed.

As the event drew closer, I had a conflict arise and needed to cancel my involvement. I thought I could reply to the automated email message and let them know. I opened the email, clicked reply, and did not get one of those unfriendly "no-reply" email addresses. It looked like I was replying to the actual sender. Great. I apologized and let her know about the change in plans. I didn't get a response, but also didn't know of another way to get in touch with her.

The event took place. I know because friends were posting pictures from it on Facebook. The following Monday, I received another email from the volunteer coordinator:

"The committee would like to send a huge thank you to all of the volunteers who came out on a chilly day to help put on another fabulous event. We truly cannot say thank you enough. This would not be possible without all of our volunteers."

Automation didn't really work here. I didn't attend. In fact, I canceled. Why was this sent? It doesn't apply to me. It's just one more email to delete.

If we take things completely literally, we could argue that they didn't thank me and weren't really talking to me. Sure, it's only talking to the "volunteers who came out," but it was sent to me, and with that alone, it's addressed to me and talking to me. Qualifying language like the copy above doesn't change that.

Automation works with care, oversight, and foresight. Remember to look at the different scenarios and think of the people receiving the messages. Are they getting the right messages at the right times? If you aren't sure, keep fiddling and testing before messages are sent.

I will continue supporting this particular nonprofit, but it's good to remember that bad automation can hurt and in some cases ruin relationships. If you can't take the time to care about messages to me, why should I care about giving you my time or money?

Automation is best when we don't notice it. And when it's noticed, it's usually not in a good way.

Your automation is working when customers don't notice

By Kelsey

Automation is nice, especially for the marketer. It saves time and money, can reduce the effort invested in tedious tasks, and potentially makes touch points more personal for the customer – unless you don't get it right. Unfortunately, when data is not quite right or automation is a bit off, that's when the disparity becomes glaringly obvious to the consumer.

Smoothly running automated marketing and well-integrated technology are like a well-maintained car – you don't pay attention to the noises as you go and everything sounds "normal." There is noise and there are interactions, but as a driver, they are exactly what you expect. You don't notice the noise of the engine as you turn it on, the whoosh of the accelerator when you push the gas pedal down, the hum of the air conditioning as it pushes cool air. You don't notice any of this noise, until it's not quite right. Then every clunk and hiss is amplified.

For businesses, when customer experience is off because of automation or technology, every ill-timed Tweet, enewsletter, display ad, mixed message, and failed communication becomes obvious and quite annoying.

When you remove human interaction from marketing distribution, for example, you lose a bit of personal touch and quality assurance. However, as organizations get bigger and bigger, that personal touch can be lost anyway.

It's a catch-22 of sorts: big marketing efforts require automation and technology to support, and the more automation and technology you add, the higher the likelihood you won't get it right for all of your consumers. If you fine-tune your efforts by downsizing automation, you won't reach as many people, potentially not being as effective. And even with more hands-on quality control, large organizations can't know if they're really getting the messaging right every time.

When it doesn't work

Extensive disclaimer: I love Target as much as the average warm-blooded, American woman – its lovely colors, bright lights, moderately priced athletic gear, sundresses, seasonal accessories, the never-knew-I-loved-that home décor section, self-checkout lanes, intimidating baby section, and bottles of kombucha. It's one of the only grocery stores in Iowa City that has kombucha exactly where I know to find it, conveniently toward the end of my usual arch through the essential departments.

In May 2016, I opened my mail to find an adorable mailer from Target. It was an eight-page booklet with a picture of a baby in a birthday hat, and it said "Let There Be Cake" on the cover. Inside were photos of birthday party decorations that made me cringe about as much as I do while perusing Pinterest, but also gave me hope that I could create such a magical scene for my son's birthday party. I also found coupons for children's books, toys, clothes, and party supplies.

Now this is a lovely use of big data. Well, the idea was. My husband and I had registered at Target when we were expecting our son in 2014. We maintained our registry through mid-2015. The problem is that this mailer came three months late. It arrived in May and my son's birthday is March 17. Target knows this, by the way. The due date was included in the registry creation. I would have loved these coupons and party ideas three months prior. Instead, I was a bit resentful that I didn't get to save purchasing party supplies and annoyed that Target had the data and didn't use it well.

Was this an irrational annoyance? Maybe. Was I back at Target picking up my essentials the next weekend? Of course.

I share this example because, had the coupon book arrived a month before my son's birthday, I probably would have leafed through the booklet, used a coupon or two, and not thought twice about the use of my registry data for evergreen marketing. Instead, they didn't get it right, and it stuck out in a very annoying way.

When it works

When automation and technology support the consumer, the experience is a beautiful melody of efficiency and effectiveness for both the user and the organization. However, when it works well, it's also nearly invisible to the user.

For example, restaurants have refined the way you're called to your table. There are four distinct approaches I've experienced in the last year:

1. You put your name in and the hostess calls you when your table is ready. You are forced to stay close by to make sure you know when you're called.

2. You put in your name and the host provides a pager. It buzzes and lights up when your table is ready. This saves you from having to sit in a crowded waiting area or worry that you missed the host calling your name across the Friday night din of conversation.

3. You put your name in and the hostess sends a text when your table is ready. This gives you a bit more radius to walk or pop in to local shops until your table is ready. It also is much slicker than the clunky pager. Not to mention, how many people have handled those devices on a busy evening during flu season?

4. You put your name in and the host writes down your name, then makes a few notes about your appearance so they can easily identify you to walk you to your seat. No hollering above the waiting area, no devices or phones to check for updates.

What option is the nicest for customers? I argue No. 3 and No. 4 provide the best experiences – one leverages automation and technology, one does not.

No. 4 requires astute observation. It takes extra effort to remember the waiting customers and engage with them personally when a table is ready. I have seen this work well in luxury restaurants where the total number of customers may be smaller than a neighborhood sports bar on a Saturday night. It is used for a smaller audience and is not always scalable based on staff and customer quantity.

The text message option is a nice feature and convenient for the customer. However, last summer I remember waiting for more than an hour and a half at a popular restaurant, only to find out that the host sent us the text message that we didn't get, and we missed our open table.

Customers usually notice technology and automation when it doesn't work. When the experience is seamless and invisible to the customer, you got it right.

A dictated medical note transformed how I view doctor-patient communication
By Kelsey

Who wants to play telephone with their medical care? I don't. Yet the traditional way of communicating and documenting a medical appointment is just that.

In June 2011, I had just finished a grueling and time-intensive four months of training for Ironman Texas (a 2.4-mile swim, 112-mile bike ride, and 26.2-mile run). During my last six weeks of training, I was in a walking boot due to a misdiagnosed stress fracture after complaining about a nagging ache in my left foot. To maintain my training, I was swimming as much as possible, riding my road bike on a trainer instead of outside, and adding sessions in the pool instead of running.

Let me tell you, six-hour indoor bike rides on Sundays are no fun. When I started the race, I hadn't run for six weeks. It was a rough day, mostly because of the heat, but I finished!

After a month of gentle recovery, I started jogging again, and the pain immediately returned. I requested a consult with an orthopedic surgeon and started researching foot and ankle specialists in the Los Angeles area, where I was living.

I'd had surgery on both feet as a 10-year old to treat a calcaneonavicular coalition. Essentially, bones in my feet had grown together and then fractured, causing pain when I ran, jumped, or played for prolonged periods. I expected that the bones in my left foot may had grown back. I remembered the feeling of achiness and sharp pain I had experienced for years as a child, and I was committed to finding an orthopedic surgeon who could get me back to Ironman-running shape if I needed another surgery.

After extensive research of physicians' bios, education, backgrounds, specialties, residencies, and fellowship experience (yes, my "type A" really comes out when looking for a doctor), I booked an appointment with Dr. Charlton, an orthopedic surgeon specializing in feet and ankles. If he could work with the New York City Ballet, USC football team, and other professional athletes, he could get me back to triathlons pain-free.

My initial visit was a surprisingly unique experience. Before seeing him, and in years since, I have never come across a provider who approached patient communication the same way.

After listening to my history, discussing my symptoms, and talking about the X-rays I had brought, he asked if there was anything else. I said no, and he retrieved his iPhone from his white coat. He then dictated a note as if he was talking to me. The experience was something like this:

"Kelsey Guetschow, a 26-year-old patient, presents today with left mid-foot and ankle pain that increases during and after exertion to include running, biking, surfing, and other high-impact activities. She just completed an Ironman, and her treatment must enable her to return to that level of activity following surgery. After reviewing the X-rays and medical history with Kelsey, I discussed the presence of bone regrowth between the calcaneal and navicular bones on her left foot. These reflect what we would expect in the previous surgery site as the original procedure, on both feet, was accomplished when Kelsey was 10 years old. Her surgery in 1995 was accomplished in the Los Angeles Children's Hospital and, following recovery, she has had no additional issues until this April. Surgical removal of new bone growth likely will resolve the discomfort in the left foot. The right foot surgery site is still completely clear as seen on the X-rays. Kelsey understands the options for surgery and treatment. We will schedule a pre-op appointment two to three weeks prior to her surgery date. She would like to schedule her surgery in the next three months, after some upcoming vacations."

At the end, he paused and asked if he had missed anything. He amended as needed, then completed the appointment.

I expect it may be difficult to understand what a wonderful experience this was. The whole time he was dictating, Dr. Charlton was making eye contact and pointing to the areas he was describing on my foot and on the X-rays so I could follow along. As a patient, what a refreshing way for a provider to communicate!

There have been too many times where, after recounting the issue in a doctor's office, they miss important details that affect medication orders or follow-up plans, and potentially patient safety.

Doctors are taxed – they see hundreds of patients a week and work incredibly long hours. They are also human and can inadvertently miss details. In many ways, they are always playing a game of telephone. The patient tells the nurse, the nurse tells the doctor, the patient tells the doctor, the doctor writes the note. For teaching hospitals, you can add in an additional step – residents. But the consequences for getting it wrong are far bigger in this game.

Mid-2016, my son had a bad chest cold that after 10 days escalated to a fever and immediate, significant demeanor changes. Since he had been hospitalized within the previous four months for severe bronchiolitis, my husband and I were concerned. My husband took him to the pediatrician for an appointment, but his primary pediatrician was not available. The doctor who was next-available did an evaluation, diagnosed him with a bacterial infection, ordered a prescription, and sent him on his way.

Two days later, my husband checked my son's MyChart record (the online medical records system) to verify the follow-up visit time and reviewed the doctor's note – it was about 50 percent inaccurate. She had noted a non-productive cough (wrong), the incorrect antibiotics currently being used for ear drainage (wrong), and a longer range for how many days the fever had been present. Now, this was not a big deal for our son, because after three days on antibiotics, he was improving. However, had he regressed and needed a follow-up visit or was admitted to the hospital, these details may have created a patient safety issue since they presented an inaccurate picture of his medical history and care.

All of these details could have been resolved had the provider followed the approach Dr. Charlton used in his orthopedic surgery clinic.

By creating a wonderful patient experience through this additional layer of communication, the provider is also completing a patient safety check on the assessment, diagnosis, and course of treatment. The provider is taking the additional step to verify that the information communicated by the patient was received correctly and appropriately documented in the medical record.

When we treat our customers well, there are unintentional, positive results – in this case, a memorable experience, improved patient safety, and likely some efficiencies in physician visit summary annotation.

Note: I contacted Dr. Charlton prior to writing this and asked how the notes he dictated on his iPhone made it into the patient record. I was hoping for a great technical solution to make the process even more efficient! He explained that their staff still types the dictated notes into the records.

Automated dictation services have not progressed enough to consistently or accurately transcribe conversations with patients. At the time of this writing, there are no agile integration options with electronic medical records.

Personalization by geography doesn't always work well
Christoph

My February 2016 trip to Germany was my first time back in Düsseldorf since smartphones, apps, and other related technological advances had entered my life.

So I was using mobile websites to check flights, apps from United States-based companies to check rentals, and other related things.

Most sites and even most apps tried to personalize the experience for me. What that typically meant was that they were serving me content in German. Some sites, like British Airways, made it super easy and obvious to change languages. Others, not so much.

One site made you click "Sprachen" which is "Languages" in German. That's only helpful if you speak

German. Now, I do speak German, but how did they all know that? I asked one company via Twitter how they knew, and they couldn't answer that. It appeared that the personalization was triggered geographically.

Google Flights, where I usually book my travel, also was showing me flight prices (for routes within the United States) in euros. They probably could know that I typically pay in dollars. Dollars were shown toward the end when I picked flights, though.

It wasn't a big deal for me, of course, but it's still worth remembering that some personalization triggers might not work for everyone.

Offline, like at the airport check-in counters, people started conversations in German, and even though I responded in German, they quickly transitioned to English when they saw my American passport. That's a good example of how it should work online as well. You have to start somewhere and then, based on user-behavior, your reactions and communications should change. I wish we were there with technology across the board.

Mass communication: customer-centric or not?
By Kelsey

Are we really customer-centric when marketing turns into a cacophony of mass communication? When we're blaring out marketing messages so broadly we only have one audience? Probably not, but is that really a problem?

In some cases, no. Certain services are universal, and really, consumers should be marketed and communicated to in the same way when there is one general audience. For example, when an airline communicates to all passengers that a flight is delayed. Everyone receives the same all-call and text message with the alert, if they signed up for text alerts when they purchased their tickets.

Or when the National Weather Service who sends out mass alerts on tornadoes, hurricanes, heavy rain, extreme wind, or whatever treat mother nature decides to share with a specific area. All customers in that area receive the same message. In this case, this mass communication is consumer-centric.

These organizations meet the needs of these consumers because they're sharing broad messages that apply to all recipients. Even if I was, for example, away for a weekend when I received the text that there was a tornado in my area, this information is still helpful so I can call to have a neighbor check on my house. The message was technically not sent to the correct audience but it is still consumer-centric because it's helpful, informative, relevant, and timely.

This kind of relevant mass communication should be rare, but many businesses wrongly use this approach. They may think, "My [service, product, etc.] applies to everyone – I should market or communicate broadly." This notion is all too common.

Broad communication usually isn't consumer-centric because you end up sharing irrelevant information with too many people. Most organizations don't refine their messaging to target specific audiences in a way that is most effective for those audiences. So as a consumer, you end up with an email full of "spammy" mass communication messages that rarely apply to you. That experience is annoying.

To be consumer-centric, organizations need to clearly identify their audiences and communicate with personal, relevant, or useful information when customers need it.

Think personalized websites, automated and personalized emails, and targeted mailers (if your organization still resorts to paper!). All of this information should be tailored to a specific individual to inform, educate, convert, and help. That type of mass communication is customer-centric.

How disruptive
By Christoph

I read a lot of stories and content on a daily basis. I'm interested in what people are saying and what the alleged latest trends are.

I find most of the content I consume through social media shares, though I do get dozens of enewsletters as well.

A well-respected content marketer shared a link to a blog I hadn't heard of. The topic sounded interesting, so I clicked to read more.

The second I started reading, I received a pop-up for the organization's enewsletter signup. Now, I know those pop-ups work, so I typically don't complain about them. I even recommend them and use them from time to time on my website.

I signed up for the enewsletter because the site came highly recommended. Once I did that, it sent me to a "welcome to the newsletter" page that explained what to expect and offered ideas for what else was good on the site.

What happened to the article I wanted to read? Could you send me back there, please? The writer is probably wondering why his visitors' time on page is so low. Hint – it's the enewsletter.

There's a fine line when converting social media visitors to enewsletter subscribers. For the readers' sake, let's stay on the right side of it. If somebody came to read something of interest to them, make sure they get the chance to read it. Being customer-centric allows the customer to do what they came to a site to do. When sites have annoying popups or popups that don't work the way they should, that's not customer-centric.

Testing can help us be customer-centric
By Christoph

A/B testing, sometimes called split testing, refers to testing an audience's reaction to a specific section of a product. Typically, A/B testing is done in email newsletters or on a website.

The A/B stands for the versions served to sample groups. Version A is served to one group of people, and version B is served to a different group. This could involve different sizes or colors of buttons on the website or different subject lines in email newsletters. Marketers will then look at the data of each sample to compare which one worked better.

A/B testing should always relate to your business and digital goals. For example, if you are trying to sell a product, you could test which copy, design, or other factor leads to more sales. If you run an informational content site, you might test what kind of content prompts visitors to read more.

A/B testing is great because, though best practices exist, one specific audience might react differently than another audience. For example, some email newsletters work better – and are opened more – when they have specific subject lines. But some audiences respond better to the same subject line each month.

Check out these examples:

Specific subject line: Ten new social media tips to increase engagement

Same subject line every month: Your monthly social media news from @ctrappe

A/B testing can help you optimize content and digital experiences for your audiences and make the experience better for them. This will pay off for you in the long-run, too.

How A/B testing might go away
By Christoph

Marketers measure what works better by doing A/B testing. For example, when we do this, 2 percent more people do whatever we wanted them to do. This testing technique works better for the masses. But "the masses" online are becoming less important while instant, relevant, one-on-one connections and experiences are becoming more important. Let's break that down some more.

The masses

Most everything online is a numbers game. The more relevant traffic you have, the higher your influence, reach, income, etc. It's still very much the typical marketing funnel approach. The more relevant people enter in the top, the more they become advocates, customers, etc. So, the importance of masses likely isn't going away.

Certainly there are exceptions, but in general, that's still the case. Think about Amazon, for example. Amazon is winning the numbers game. The masses know about them and buy things from the site. But they are hailed as a company that gets personalization right. They know me so well that it's hard not to buy their recommendations, which are truly personalized to me. It's those one-on-one interactions that make the Amazon experience customer-centric – and trying to A/B test personalized experiences would be ineffective.

A/B testing is helpful and works in the pre-personalization era. In a web world where content is truly personalized, A/B testing in the traditional sense won't matter because it's not about moving the masses, but about moving the individual.

One-on-one relationships

When two people have a relationship, they know things about each other – likes, dislikes, flaws, strengths, etc. Many of us, when we choose to, adjust our styles to the other person. The same concept can apply online when it comes to digital experiences.

Instead of marketers testing what increases conversions from the masses, we should work on knowing our customers and potential customers better and trying to have a meaningful relationship. What's meaningful, of course, depends on each relationship and is a bit of a fluid concept.

So that means the content and experience presented to me is very different from those that are presented to you. They know so much about me that the experiences are completely optimized and super relevant to me. And by super relevant, I don't mean that it's only optimized to get me to buy more. It's optimized to help me – the customer.

Of course, marketers knowing things about me also can be dangerous, because they can use that information to get me to buy, buy, buy. And sometimes it's about buying something and sometimes it's not. The marketer of the future uses customer information for the customer's benefit.

Testing in the future

This is one of the more debated points I've made at conferences and in workshops. People tell me that this will never be possible, and some have called me crazy. "Testing will never go away! Never." I wonder if people whose jobs were automated in the last few decades said the same thing. And maybe in a perfect, futuristic world, who knows if we'll ever get to a level of personalization where no testing is needed. Or maybe, testing will move from testing the masses to testing personal experiences. Some days I get served the A test and some days the B test. That could be very relevant to me, the consumer, if it's used to make the experience better for me.

Testing: good for business, better for the customer
By Kelsey

Here's a topic in which Christoph and I diverge, more in facets of opinion than overall stance.

When you are working with a team on a product or customer experience, you have to back up your opinions with data. To get the data, you need to test. You have to understand the experience of the masses. For now, organizations can easily test a consumer's digital experience through A/B or multivariate testing. You aggregate the results of those tests and general experiences to pinpoint refinements that can be made for the masses. This approach provides opportunities for helpful customer-focused insights and experience improvements.

I agree with Christoph that many future trends will be around testing to refine the individual experience. However, I think that this kind of refinement can be done through adjusting your approach to testing the masses – especially when we do have the ability to segment these people by general behavioral patterns, goal completions, personas, and more.

Testing can be arduous. Too many people jump into the testing phase without properly completing the planning and strategy required to complete a successful test.

There are a few ways you can start to hone your mass A/B testing to a more personalized approach. First, if you already have a question in mind, approach the test with the traditional scientific method – question, research, hypothesize, test, draw conclusions, repeat. The same is true whether you are testing the best way to engage a customer through a marketing channel or the effectiveness of a web design layout.

In 2016, I read a brilliant blog post by Craig Kistler titled "Improving Conversion Rates with Better A/B Tests." It was posted on the InVision Blog.[3] In the article, Kistler advocates for evaluation of web designs through A/B testing to improve conversion rates, and that to do this effectively, it needs to be repeatable.

---

[3] http://blog.invisionapp.com/improving-conversion-rates-ab-tests/

I referred back to the article when I was evaluating a web design the following week. There were a couple of elements I just didn't like about the site, but I couldn't explain why. When the boss says, "I don't like it," but the data says "it" is working well, you have to push back with the data. If the boss says, "I don't like the color of that layout," switch the color, do an A/B test on the options, and present which outperforms the other.

Even better, many technology platforms now allow for multivariate testing. That means you can test more options than A and B. You can test options C, D, and E at the same time and conclusively say which variations and combination of the digital experience works best.

By definition, this is testing to the masses. However, in reality, it's testing individual user experiences and combining the results to provide conclusive recommendations into overall user trends and effectiveness. Use the data to identify what your users prefer.

Always consider that data can be manipulated to make it tell your story. In assessing a design, a policy, or a customer experience, we have to keep in mind that the most effective option for the customer should be the right option, and we must check our biases at the door.

I'm sure we all have seen documentaries that present an incredibly convincing story for one side of an argument. In fact, in 2016, the Tribeca Film Festival pulled the film "Vaxxed" from the festival after claims in the feature, and data with which the creators founded their claims, were proven largely unfounded and inaccurate.

When you are working through a hypothesis, especially one related to customer experience, you also have to be sure you're solving the right problem.

I did an evaluation of a website where the form completion rates were not as high as we were expecting. The form was rather long, so we immediately recommended that we test cutting the total number of fields. This helped some, but we discovered we weren't asking the right question.

At the same time as the initial test, we also had placed some tracking on the site to record user behavior. Watching some of the individual user recordings, we saw users struggling with filling in a field that should have been pre-populated based on the previous page the user viewed.

Why were we making them fill this in? We already knew what preference they wanted. A quick adjustment made this an auto-fill option and completion rates rose 13 percent in the first three weeks. It helped the organization increase their digital ROI, but in the end, it was a much easier process for the customer.

Testing helps you solve problems, illuminate blind spots, and refine the customer experience. Testing may go away as automation continues to improve, but we should never eliminate the opportunity to validate and refine the customer's experience and in turn build lasting relationships and loyalty.

How many emails is too many?
By Christoph

Sending enewsletters is one of the most effective customer-conversion tactics. Email is not dead at all. Even though sometimes we'd like it to die. Ha.

When done well, sending emails to our customers can help us be of more value to them while it also helps our business. But how many is too many?

I wondered how many enewsletters I personally get and how to decide which ones are valuable and relevant to me. So I ran a little test.

Every enewsletter is required to have an unsubscribe function, so I thought the easiest way to track how many I get would be to filter all emails with the word "unsubscribe" into a special folder. Between September 1 and September 6, 2015, that folder had 100 emails in it. In just a touch over five days, I received 100 enewsletters. Around 19 per day.

Wow. That seems super high. Did I read them all? Nope! I even unsubscribed from some. But I read the ones that:

- Have content that is super relevant to me
- Arrive at the right time for me and when I actually have time to read them
- Come from somebody I know and trust, even if just online
- Don't end up in my spam folder
- Don't always sell to me

A combination of these points make enewsletters relevant to me. The other day, I received 12 at the same time. Needless to say, I didn't have the time to read all 12. I skimmed one and the others went into the trash. Not necessarily because the content wasn't good (I have no idea if it was!) but because of the less-than-great timing. I was too busy for 12 emails.

Sometimes, relevant content is something new – something the reader didn't know they wanted until they saw it. New things surprise us and pull us in. If a newsletter just tells me what I already read 42 times yesterday on Twitter, what's the point?

Enewsletters are a high-converting tactic and get read more than the gazillion Tweets flying by us, but just like all other channels, the content and everything around how it's delivered needs to be right for our audiences.

If it's not, it's just more noise. And irrelevant noise simply gets ignored.

What can we do to make enewsletters more relevant?

- Know our audiences.
- Have a content strategy in place, like we do for all other channels.
- Keep content simple.
- Test to see what works and what doesn't.
- Include calls-to-action that count, and don't make people click just to drive a metric.
- Send people to optimized landing pages when you do make people click.
- Make sure the email works on mobile devices. Responsive design is an easy solution.

Enewsletters are a great way to connect with our audiences and communities. But, just like other channels, good enough is no longer good enough. Just a touch better than others isn't good enough anymore, either. More relevant, unique content is where the difference will be made.

How to Prove Success

Measuring the wrong thing
By Christoph

Proving success can be tricky, especially when leaders expect results the moment something new starts. Overnight success takes longer than overnight!

And sometimes we pick the wrong metrics. When we do, it's OK to admit that and change them. Let me give you an example from the digital realm, where everyone tries to measure everything.

Some marketers still use the number of pages people view on one website visit as a measure of success. The theory goes that the more pages people click to view, the more engaged they are.

Certainly, I want people to click all around my site and read more of my stuff. But a low page-per-visit number can indicate a good customer experience. It depends.

Let's say a visitor comes to my site, finds what they came for, and leaves. The pages-per-visit count certainly will be low, and the bounce rate might be high as well. Oh no, people are viewing only one page! But they were happy with their visit because they got what they needed.

I couldn't tell you what my average pages-per-visit number and bounce rate is on my blog. But I can tell you – without looking it up – how many monthly visitors I see and how many people have come through my website to hire me to speak or for digital marketing strategy. Those goals matter to me because I know that the bigger my relevant audience (community) gets, the more likely it is for me to make an impact for them and me.

Bounce rate and pages-per-visit are something to keep in mind and review. But here are some reasons why your content strategy may be successful even if your bounce rate is high and your pages-per-visit metric is low.

1. Goals are being completed

People come to sites for a specific reason – to satisfy a need and leave. For example, when somebody comes to my speaking page, I don't necessarily want them to keep reading other posts. I want them to decide whether I'm a good match for their event and hire me to speak.

2. Social traffic to blog posts is strong

People come to blogs from social to read an article that was shared on social media. It's nice if they read more, but they completed their goal by landing on your page.

Consider a retargeting campaign on social media to get them coming back again, and maybe to encourage them to sign up for your enewsletter.

3. Clicking around may signal issues

Let's say somebody comes to your site and visits a lot of pages. Maybe they can't find what they're looking for but haven't given up yet. Pages visited will be up, but satisfaction? Not so much.

4. Maybe they were just bored

Sometimes I just aimlessly click around the web – usually on social networks. That's not a sign of engagement. It's a sign of boredom.

Goals are great, and it's important to have engagement goals. But let's be careful what we measure and why. Action isn't always engagement, and some alleged engagement metrics don't show engagement at all.

Thinking about your goals and how to measure them is important but easily can be overthought. Many projects take time, including changing to a customer-centric mindset.

This quick story comes to mind. I once talked to a global company's CEO who wanted to try storytelling to stand out in the market place. He said, "We want content marketing to generate revenue before we fund it too much."

Huh? Ugh, I didn't reply with "huh," but I wanted to. This kind of statement and attitude isn't that uncommon, unfortunately. Prove to me that it works before I invest the amount it takes to actually make it work.

Now, don't get me wrong. You can do content marketing on a shoestring. I've done it before and still do from time to time. But usually this tactic is best used by small businesses and startups.

So I asked how much he expects to make from this in year one. He gave me a number. I told him the project for year one would cost 15 percent of that number. Seemed shoestring to me. Ha.

On the other side of the "effort vs. value" discussion is the often inaccurate "projecting and guessing" game.

If I do X and invest this much time, I will get Y. It's guaranteed! Unfortunately, hardly anything is guaranteed.

I likely would never have started blogging or speaking had I overanalyzed everything first. I just started doing it. **The best plan is moving toward a declared goal.**

Don't get me wrong, I change things all the time. If something isn't working or doesn't align with my declared goals, it gets the ax. Done. It's out of here or gets adjusted to keep moving me toward my goals.

Sometimes value can be guessed or something can be dismissed without trying. Many times it can't. I've been on many projects where success happened and teams learned something because they focused more on doing than analyzing what they could or should be doing.

You could have hit that breakthrough in the next minute – the one you didn't spend. The only way to win the game is by playing it, not by sitting on the sidelines analyzing what may or may not happen.

Measure what matters, not everything you can
By Kelsey

Big data. Information intelligence. Data cloud. Analytics. Customer profiling. Customer satisfaction. So many options to understand your business and the factors influencing your successes or shortfalls.

I get hundreds of emails a week from sales people who have "the best" data warehouse or customer insight tool. Their tag lines convey a message of: Measure everything! Know all facets of your business and customer! It goes on and on.

At business conferences, there is always a learning track or keynote toting impactful, groundbreaking transformations from big data. In exhibition areas, marketing materials pop with analytics, data, results, and insights. Big data is screaming at businesses, urging measurement to drive results. The deafening noise is so loud you easily can miss opportunities to capture insights that matter most.

Ask the question: What customer interactions most poignantly affect our business and customers? Measure those. Measure things that can move the dial for your business. But the conundrum of access to so much data is: "what dial do I move?"

Focus on using your insights to improve and align customer conversions and customer experience. Both are multifaceted, and both are unique for different businesses and across industries. Use due diligence, be curious, and ask where, how, when your customers are converting and what their journey is like along the way.

Customer conversions matter just as much, if not more than, customer experience. Both build the business and increase revenue, but the latter also establishes loyalty and reputation. These are two less tangible business elements that are harder to achieve, measure, and correct once tarnished.

Analyze data through the lens of a story. What is the data telling you? What story does it unveil about the customer experience you are creating or inhibiting? When you dive deep into data, it can be hard to resurface to soak in the surrounding landscape and understand the implications. Continual curiosity will drive you through lengthy data analysis. Have discipline to regularly float above the noise and ask what the data is telling you and what story you're missing. Use these answers to improve customer interactions and their experiences.

Never before have we had so much access to nearly unlimited customer behavioral insights. But let's not lose sight of the unique opportunity to use data to propel customer experience into an increasingly positive state.

Interact with your organization like you are a customer
By Kelsey

How many times have you struggled to navigate a customer experience? Have you tried to figure out how to get an appointment scheduled, a prescription refilled, a reservation changed, or a return processed, only to feel like you're banging your head against the wall, sarcastically wondering whether the process could get any more inconvenient?

As organizational leaders, we often focus too minutely on process, requirements, or policy and lose sight of the rippling implications of customer experience. It is easier to make our customer interactions bend to our requirements instead of accommodating for a more positive customer experience.

Years ago, I was working in a large ambulatory clinic. Six providers made up our primary care department, and they always were booked to capacity. The front desk staff was often shorthanded and behind on checking in patients, answering internal phone calls, and completing registration paperwork.

Clinical leadership cut scheduling appointments from the staff's responsibilities and moved scheduling to our call center. The new process required a lot of training and took longer than a usual check-in. This inadvertently created an unfortunate customer flow.

A typical patient experience went something like this:

- Wait in line to check in
- Show ID and verify contact information with the front desk staff
- Be called back for your appointment by a medical technician or nurse

- Have vitals and brief history taken, then let the technician record your complaints, verify your current medication list, and present your information to the provider
- Wait for provider to come in, complete the appointment, and recommend a follow-up visit
- Stop by the front desk to schedule a follow-up and find out the front desk can't help.
- Get directed to a phone in the lobby to call the contact center and schedule the follow-up appointment
- Call the appointment line and wait on hold for five minutes (ironically, the call center is located 150 feet from the phone where you are on hold)
- Connect finally and schedule the follow-up and depart the building

This sounds so inconvenient for the patient it's almost unbelievable, but this was the established and accepted policy. And there were some brilliant people running the clinic. However, one thing I noticed was that no internal staff completely followed the regulated patient flow.

Instead of having people wait in line to check in, the front desk would recognize them and check them in. I remember getting emails saying I was checked in a few minutes before I needed to walk down to the lobby.

When staff needed an appointment, they would walk to the call center and sit with a clerk to schedule, even at peak call times. I remember having friends stop by my office after their appointment to say hello. If they made an annoyed comment that the front desk wouldn't schedule their follow-up, I would open the appointment system and do it for them.

When you work within an organization, you rarely, if ever, have to completely navigate all facets of the experience as external customers.

There are always easier ways to accomplish a transaction when you work within the organization – exceptions that you can implement to make your experience easier, conveniences not afforded to the regular customer.

If we don't engage with our own organization like an external customer, we miss opportunities for improvement. We don't see the pain points we are creating and forcing our customers to endure. We ignore inconveniences as acceptable or necessary annoyances because they better support our policies instead of objectively quantifying them from the customer perspective.

The next time you need to accomplish something within your organization, go about it like you are a customer. Walk through all of the steps they have to, then analyze what can improve. You may be surprised by what you find.

The exercise will illuminate how you may be making customers work instead of providing a loyalty-building interaction, or it can reveal how you already are customer-centric.

Payoff for Doing It Well

Long-term payoff
By Christoph

My 18-month-old daughter uses the iPhone like she has taken an "iPhones for babies" class. Of course, there's no such class (I think) and iPhones are designed so well they don't need explanation. You pick them up — including babies, apparently — and start using them.

Unfortunately, not everything in our lives is designed well. When you have to post a lot of signs or directions, that's usually a sign of bad design. Not always, but often.

I once went to an actual store because I had to buy something and needed it now. No Amazon Prime this time. There was a long line of customers waiting for the two cashiers, who were at the two registers on the right. There was another station on the left that looked pretty much like the others.

A third employee, presumably a cashier, walked up to the empty station. A woman in front of me looked at the employee and said, "Oh no, sorry. This looks like a register, but it's not. Please go over this way." She pointed at the two cashiers. It was a bit awkward, as you may imagine.

The person who wasn't a cashier started working on something at the third station, and the customers shuffled over to the two actual cashiers.

Whoever designed this setup most likely had a reason behind it. Maybe that station was for a supervisor who needed to be close to the cashiers. Maybe it's where people return merchandise. I don't know.

But to the customers, it felt strange. It felt out of place. And it definitely wasn't customer-centric.

Unexpected benefits of great customer experience
By Kelsey

Organizations know they should focus on customer experience. Unfortunately, sometimes it's easier not to.

Certain companies are what I call essential services. If you offer an essential service, customers still have other alternatives, but most of the time they're limited.

Examples of essential services include:

- **Rural highway gas stations:** You don't have to stop if you have gas, but if you need gas, this business may be your only option.
- **Emergency rooms:** When you're having a true medical emergency, you go to the closest ER. Your life is more important than driving an extra 15 or 20 minutes to a preferred hospital.
- **Healthcare subspecialty clinics or doctors:** This is when a specialty is offered on a limited basis in your area, or anywhere. This mainly applies to incredibly subspecialized providers and organizations – Cancer Centers of America, Mayo Clinic, Dana-Farber Cancer Institute, etc. People travel for care around the world for treatment because these doctors and clinics are the best or only option for incredibly rare or advanced conditions.
- **Specialty car repair:** Special parts and tools are needed to repair and maintain rare or luxury cars. Think Tesla.
- **Internet/cable providers:** If you live in a small community or rural area, you often have only one to three options for internet or cable.

When companies provide essential services, they can approach customer experience in one of two ways: 1) It doesn't matter – customers have to come to us anyway or 2) we prioritize customer experience to build long-term customer loyalty, which can change an essential service into an exclusive experience.

Unfortunately, organizations fail when they discount the long-term influence or repercussive impacts of a bad customer experience.

In 2012, my grandmother was rushed to an ER in Los Angeles. The hospital was a mid-size facility in a nice neighborhood. When I arrived, she had already been there for four hours, going through tests and labs while they stabilized her breathing.

The scene I found was disgusting. I walked into the treatment room where she was being held pending admission and was immediately hit by the putrid smell of feces. Quickly realizing it was coming from the restroom attached to her room, and seeing the cause of the odor through the door, I put on gloves and grabbed a trash bag from the aid cart sitting in the hallway. I bagged up the trash that was full of dirty adult diapers and soiled clothing, all the while wondering how no one else had bothered to take care of this all afternoon.

I then went to sit down next to her bed only to find soiled sheets and a dirty patient gown crumpled in the corner by her monitors (they were not hers). Again, I put on gloves, collected the laundry, and disposed of it with other soiled linens in the hallway. Finally, sitting down with her, I asked how she was feeling and received an overview of the day's events from her caretakers. Quickly realizing she had not had any food since arrival and it was now almost 9 p.m., I walked back into the hallway, found a medical technician who apologetically located what he could (apparently the cafeteria was closed). He brought in a sandwich and some containers of fruit.

Had basic patient experience been pushed to the side because she didn't have another option for treatment at the time? How hard would it have been to address the obvious needs to make her experience better?

Having worked in a trauma center in a war zone, I understand better than most what a busy day looks like in an ER. I'm incredibly understanding that medical needs come before experience needs, but often they're more closely tied than people think. All of those experience problems I shared about my grandmother's ER stay were actually significant concerns for patient safety and infection control.

The day after I visited my grandmother in the ER, I contacted the hospital's patient safety representative through a phone call and an online concern form, hoping it was an instance of "we can't address what we don't know." I received no response.

When you run a medical practice like plastic surgery, where there is high competition and patients want the best experience, provider, amenities, and location, it's easy to see why focusing on patient experience matters – it generates more business. But when providing an essential service like Emergency care, your patients need you right now and there is rarely competition. This is an opportunity to create a lasting customer advocate.

You build trust and loyalty when you treat patients well beyond their medical needs. When patients are in the ER, they usually are at their most vulnerable. By considering their whole experience during the course of care, when they do need additional treatment for a non-essential service, they'll be back because they know you'll take good care of them.

In healthcare, when we consider the patient experience as we go, we also improve our overall quality of care. It's a win-win for everyone.

Getting reviews
By Christoph

Influencer marketing and outreach. Brand ambassador programs. Social media amplification. And any other buzz phrase you can think of to help brands get our stories shared.

All these tactics actually work. But they can and will backfire when the product stinks.

Marketing isn't usually in charge of product development or customer service, but often is in charge of content, product, and traditional marketing programs. And marketing crap is still marketing crap.

Sometimes I talk with clients about ways to amplify their product and customer service stories. And many times I get this: "But what if it's a negative experience, and they share that publicly?"

OMG. A negative experience. Sounds like life, which is made up of positives and negatives. Intermixing them actually makes us look – dare I say – human and more relatable.

When negative stories are shared:

- Acknowledge them
- Show understanding (empathy)
- Address and fix them as applicable

But, I get it. **We want people to share our positive stories.** Here's how to do that:

Create positive experiences for them in the field. Yes, those front desk clerks are members of your brand reputation team. You may not know their names, and they don't report to you. It may sound complicated, because it is – but it really isn't at the same time.

How do you scale good customer service? Everyone offer great customer service now. Go!

Of course, leadership shouldn't create rules to make this more difficult, and if the product is bad, we should fix the product first. Good customer service likely can't save a crappy product.

So how do you scale creating a good product? Create a good product to begin with.

And when people share a negative OR positive story about your brand online, respond as you would offline. If somebody comes up to me and says, "Nice tie," I would thank them. The same concept should apply online. Some exemptions might be huge brands (so not most of us) who get mentioned continually.

Let me give you an example of a positive brand story that moved from offline to online. In October 2016, I was in Toronto for a day to talk content marketing and storytelling. I stayed downtown in the fancy Delta Hotel, a Marriott property.

The front desk clerk was nice and said, "Thanks for being a Silver Elite Member (which means I stay with Marriott often). I was able to get you a complimentary upgrade to our luxury suite."

Cool. Thanks. My phone was ready to Instagram some photos.

That suite, which overlooked the convention center and the Blue Jays baseball stadium, was nicer and bigger than my college apartment. How delightful!

I called the desk later and asked how much the room typically costs. They said it was around $700, and that I'd gotten it because they'd run out of regular rooms. Of course, I only learned that because I was nosy. Once a reporter, always a reporter.

Does that mean we always have to give customers something for free? No, but your product has to rock, the experience has to at least live up to expectations, and sometimes it must exceed them.

Brand reputation is a team sport and crosses all departments. Act like a team, offer things that matter, and work together. There's no way to get there alone.

What online reviews should we respond to?

Responding to online reviews shows a certain level of customer-centric belief. Everyone has license to be a critic, and people have the right to participate, share their experiences, and help others in our communities make better decisions.

Of course, with people sharing their opinions and experiences (real and perceived), questions of responding to all these reviews come up:

- Should we respond to only negative reviews or all reviews?
- Who will do the responding?
- Why do people leave reviews in the first place?

Most of the time, people leave reviews when they feel strongly about something. They're either upset, dissatisfied, or super happy.

Think about the stories we share with friends. We don't say, "I had an average experience." We typically say, "Can you believe this? It was so bad. Here are the details." Or we might say, "I'm in love with this company. Their service is the best. They're so helpful."

People share the best and the worst, for the most part. I have seen neutral reviews from time to time, but they don't help me make up my mind to buy or engage with an organization. So that's something to keep in mind.

Correct issues for the audience

I look at reviews as an extension of life. Our lives used to be offline only. Now they extend online.

When somebody gives us a compliment offline, we respond. We don't just stand there, say nothing, and ignore it. That would be rude.

I think of responding online similarly. If somebody talks to me, I respond. If my service caused a problem, I'll fix it.

Once, I was presenting at a conference and gave away books to people who participated in a session. I changed the rules along the way.

One person rated my session six out of six, but also called me on the book thing afterwards. The person sitting next to her did as well. They said they should have gotten a free copy after the rule change. That was true. And I missed it, unfortunately, during the session.

These conversations were through instant message, so not public. Either way, it didn't leave a good impression with them. However, I took the time to respond and correct the situation. I apologized and explained myself, then sent them signed copies of my book. #Done.

How to respond to negative reviews

Responding to negative reviews is no different in concept. First try to identify and understand the main problem the person addressed.

Then respond appropriately and with empathy, but never with a canned message. Always customize your responses, even when the base comes from a standard response.

Move the conversation to a private channel when necessary, but keep in mind that not all conversations need to be private – even negative conversations. However, if an answer would release private information, it certainly needs to move to another channel. The key is to acknowledge the issue, empathize, and respond quickly with a solution.

Responding to reviews and mentions online can help strengthen our brands. It can be harder for large brands. For small brands, the owner might be able to handle responding, or a small team can. The larger the brand, the more people you'll need to hire to respond.

Airlines do this well. Delta and American Airlines, for example, respond quickly to public messages. Delta even says in ads that they do this.

Reviews, blog comments, and social media questions fall into similar models for me. When people talk to us – positively or negatively – we should respond. It's the nice and right thing to do. It shows that we listen, participate, and care.

Even more online communication issues
By Christoph

The way many companies communicate online is interesting. Some don't, some are too markety, and many forget about the importance of accurate information.

Markety communication

Much of the content I read on websites is so self-congratulatory, back-patting, superlative-driven that it puts even the perfect social media lives Kelsey mentioned to shame.

Everything is oh-so perfect! I'm sure you know what I'm talking about. It's sentences and phrases like these:

- We are the best in our field.
- Our oh-so innovative approach.
- This machine is top-of-the-line/state-of-the-art/etc.
- This is the only facility this side of the Mississippi River that does X, Y, or Z.

I'm not totally against using terms or phrases like this, but when we do, we need to back them up. If you tell me you're innovative, also show me why and how.

If you state that you're the only one doing one thing or another, tell me how you know. Who declared that, or is it personal knowledge/perception? Even if it's personal perception, that's still good to know. I don't know anyone else who talks about storytelling and how it relates to content marketing the way I do. As far as I know, that's a true statement.

In general, it seems to me that those awesome-sounding terms are a leftover from marketing copy. Maybe brochures. Maybe news releases. Maybe there was a time when people thought that was good storytelling.

Edit superlatives like you are running out of words. If it's absolutely required to use them, show why they are true. There are ways to do that:

- Share a customer story.
- Share third-party data, like from a national association or governing body.
- Document somebody else using that awesome term to describe your organization. I didn't start calling myself an expert until others started calling me one.

Sharing stories by people who actually were impacted by a service showing your brand's innovation has power, but only when their stories are believable. I'm not saying they're lying, but some "customer stories" shared by brands – even when they are totally legit – can come off as fake. Even when it says "actual human" under their name.

Another way to get those customer testimonials is to catch them when people share them on their own social media channels or blogs. Those stories usually are shared for personal reasons and often appear genuine and authentic, because they are. People even make decisions based on those stories. Same with reviews. Catch good reviews and see if you can amplify them, with permission, of course.

Measuring success
By Christoph

In general, customers are people who buy things from you. But they don't always buy. Sometimes they're your advocate or feedback buddy. Either way, you have to have something to sell for customer service to be important. Without it, you might be a nice person, but it's not customer service.

There are a multitude of ways to determine the success of your customer service, and all of these metrics matter:

- Your net promoter score: An official measurement that shows how many people advocate for you and how many speak negatively about you.
- Anecdotes: They get a bad rap, but collect enough of them and you can get a good idea of what works and what doesn't.
- Customer and employee happiness: Are people willing to leave you positive references and reviews?

And, of course, revenue. There are ways to make a lot of money without being customer-centric. For example, if you're the only one who fulfills a need or has the current stronghold on a market. I say "current stronghold" because things change.

However, delighting your customers can help you make a lot of money and create long-term customer relationships. This doesn't mean the customer is always right. It means that you solve your customer's problem at a price that lets you both win, and you do it in a way that makes you both feel good about the relationship.

Creating customer advocates
By Kelsey

Marketing channels are saturated. As a customer, it can be exhausting to consume the amount of information companies push out every day.

Think about it. In any given day, a customer is likely to:

- Check email: A barrage of the hottest weekly updates, offers, or newsletters, particularly on Monday mornings.
- Scroll through social media: Promoted Facebook posts, Tweets, etc.
- Drive along a major road: Traditional billboards scream to pull over now, shop here, eat here!
- Get their regular mail: A pile of ads and mailing promotions, including catalogues from the last place they purchased a wedding gift for a friend.
- Watch TV: At least 15 minutes of commercials in an hour show, and even if you're on an internet-based provider like Hulu or Netflix, there are still promotions for the next best show or product.
- Listen to the radio or a music app: More commercials and promotions.
- Check a weather app: Banner ads across the top.

That's a lot of marketing in one day! When you start paying attention to all the marketing noise, so much is all about hype. As a customer, all that marketing is so loud. It's sharing the next big thing, the best deal (ever!), the newest restaurant, the best, the best, the best. And it all blends together.

The ads we remember and the companies that leave a mark are those that offer personal messages and connect with us. Effective marketing is about telling people a story of why you care, how your company can serve them, and how you can help them.

When you stop focusing on the hype of how to get more customers or how to we sell more and start focusing on the connection, you'll build long-term relationships, loyal customers, and customer advocates.

There are three things I will never try without a referral from a friend or acquaintance: a hair stylist, a house cleaning service, or a car repair shop. I always ask around, get a referral, and hear what others recommend based on their experiences.

In today's digital world, where online reviews are available for everything from doctors to dog kennels, one could argue that the need for in-person customer advocates has gone away. But no matter how many reviews are posted online, people talk.

They connect with one another and share their experiences. They recommend or warn friends and acquaintances about companies. They do all of this in person, where companies don't have the opportunity to respond like they do online.

Word of mouth isn't going away. Building relationships with your customer advocates secures organic marketing for your organization. By delighting customers, they'll market for you without the hype and noise. Instead, they'll market in the most personal and meaningful way – through sharing their personal, authentic experiences.

Conclusion

As our reader and customer, we hope you enjoyed the insights, stories, and examples of how you can get customer-focused. We're committed to helping organizations make lasting and meaningful connections with their customers.

Regardless of industry, customers are why we do what we do, and their experiences are important. Organizations and individuals have the power to affect the lives of their customers.

Take what you learned, apply these insights, and let us know how you succeed.

Good luck!

Thanks for reading

Get Customer-Focused

We look forward to your review of our book on Amazon, or reach us directly on Twitter at @ctrappe or @kguetschow.